Converting to an
Eco-Friendly Home

THE COMPLETE HANDBOOK

PAUL HYMERS

NEW HOLLAND

DEDICATION

For my family, Melanie, Karina and Rochelle – who have allowed me to forget them far too often, and for Harry Perkins and his generation – best wishes for the future.

Reprinted in 2008
First published in 2006 by New Holland Publishers (UK) Ltd
Garfield House
86-88 Edgware Road
London W2 2EA
www.newhollandpublishers.com

3 5 7 9 10 8 6 4

ISBN 978 1 84537 406 8

Editors: Ruth Hamilton and Ian Penberthy
Designer: Casebourne Rose Design Associates
Illustrator: Sue Rose
Editorial direction: Rosemary Wilkinson
Front cover photograph: Courtesy of Solar Twin Ltd (www.solartwin.com)

Printed and bound by Kyodo Printing Co, Singapore

ACKNOWLEDGEMENTS

Thanks to Carl for support and technical advice on all matters electrical. And to all those engaged in eco-friendly improvements who have allowed me to share in their experience and enthusiasm.

DECLARATION

The views expressed in this book are those of the author and do not necessarily reflect those of his employers.

Contents

Introduction

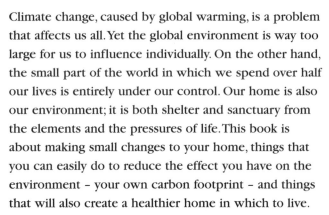

Climate change, caused by global warming, is a problem that affects us all. Yet the global environment is way too large for us to influence individually. On the other hand, the small part of the world in which we spend over half our lives is entirely under our control. Our home is also our environment; it is both shelter and sanctuary from the elements and the pressures of life. This book is about making small changes to your home, things that you can easily do to reduce the effect you have on the environment – your own carbon footprint – and things that will also create a healthier home in which to live.

One day, no doubt, we won't have to think about making 'green' choices or increasing our environmental awareness, because those choices will have been made already and that awareness will have become second nature. The problem is that 'one day' may be some time in the future.

In the meantime, while adapting your lifestyle may not be easy, adapting your home is relatively straightforward. Simple alterations that improve insulation and lighting, cleanse the air, reduce water consumption and increase energy efficiency will soon pay for themselves. More ambitious changes can free you, in part, from the grip of power and fuel companies, setting you on the road to self-sufficiency and saving you money for years to come.

Most importantly, you will not only create a better environment for your home, but also a better home for the environment.

CHAPTER ONE

Light

An eco-friendly home is a home blessed with light.

Light brings with it security, serenity and good health. It reacts with chemicals in our skin to create vitamin D, feeding our bodies with calcium, but much more than that it engenders a sense of well-being that feeds our minds, and lifts our hearts and our spirits. It is no coincidence that when homes are judged for fitness under public health laws, the amount of daylight afforded to rooms is measured. A minimum of ten per cent window area to floor area has been considered the minimum for habitable rooms for some time, and if you've ever had to spend time in a basement away from daylight, you'll understand why that is. With advances in glazing, such as Low-e glazing (see diagram, right) we can stretch that ratio to 33 per cent to give us the best possible exposure to natural light.

Improving natural light indoors

Of course the very best form of light is natural light, and to be truly green you would have to live by it alone, but that would be a little restrictive. For the times when natural light is insufficient for our requirements, we have to create light artificially, and it seems we need a lot of artificial light these days. But before we get into that, we can look to see if we are making the best possible use of the daylight that is free to us all.

When the first glazed windows were used in the 16th century, they were formed from tiny panes that were joined together with thick strips of lead. Daylight had a hard job to penetrate them. The

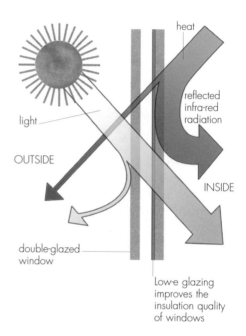

Low-e glazing improves the insulation quality of windows

Low-e glazing

Georgians made huge windows to accommodate the fact that small panes of cast glass were still being used between substantial timber bars, and it wasn't until 1838, when the rolling process of glass manufacture was invented, that windows had more glass than frame. Rolling made it possible to make larger panes. The Victorians gradually increased their size in the styling of their sash windows, which once had contained as many as eight panes in each sash, leading to just two in the Edwardian era. Edwardian homes that haven't since been modernized with plastic double-glazed units are flooded with daylight because of them.

Windows are still large to this day, but

5

by a strange twist of fate, the method of supporting the glazing is still reducing the amount of light they let through. To avoid the chore of repainting window frames, we have switched from wood to plastic, and to improve insulation, double-glazing has become standard. The gap between the panes has grown progressively wider, and now two panes of 4 mm glass are used in most, with a 20 mm cavity between them.

PVC-u replacement windows have been installed at a phenomenal rate since the 1980s, but plastic isn't as strong as timber, and to compensate for that the framework has to be thicker. The sections are deep and chunky, and on a standard double-casement window measuring 1.2 m wide by 1.05 m high, the glass can be account for less than 75 per cent of the whole area.

It is worse than you think. The single thin sheets of glass used by the Edwardians might have been terrible for keeping in the heat, but they were excellent for letting in daylight. Almost all ultra-violet light can pass through single glazing, but only 75 per cent can pass through a 20 mm double-glazed unit, while a triple-glazed unit offers significantly worse performance. Consequently, larger areas of glass are needed to compensate for that light loss.

To put it simply, we need bigger windows if we are to enjoy the benefit of daylight fully. The problem is that even the best triple glazing can lead to a significant heat loss compared to an insulated wall. At best, it offers an insulation value that is slightly worse than a cavity wall

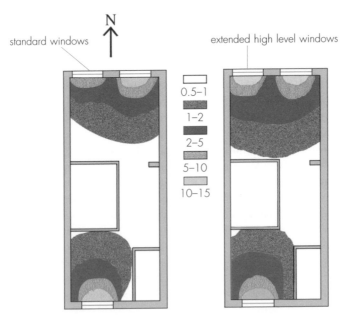

Floor plans of two identical terraced homes showing the extent to which daylight can penetrate rooms when different windows are installed

comprising two skins of bricks and no insulation. The best double-glazed windows are comparable to a solid one-brick wall in the rate of heat loss.

There is some balancing to be done here: as well as sizing windows, their orientation lies at the core of the problem.

In spite of the fact that light travels at a constant and incredible speed, it is easily deflected. Daylight arriving on vertical walls does so at an angle; some of it is reflected, some becomes distorted by double glazing and some makes it into the room just behind the window. High-level windows and windows that are tall rather than wide are much better for lighting a room, although ultimately a combination of both is best. Patio doors are great for letting natural light into a room, but traditional thinking in house design has restricted most homes to one pair, which tend to be stuck in the back somewhere and covered with a conservatory later.

My guess is that in most homes there is at least one window that could be replaced by a pair of glazed doors, without having to widen the opening or disturb the lintel over it. All that's required is to cut out the wall beneath it, install the doors and make good the reveals. Of course if extra doors will prove to be an unwanted security risk downstairs, full-height glazing can be used instead with openable vents as required. Full-height glazing is in architectural fashion at the moment, and many new-home builders are installing glass that stretches from floor to ceiling. To do this in an existing home requires some structural alteration. Better to stick with your existing window openings and extend beneath them.

Upstairs, you can do the same with fixed toughened glass or opening doors and a 'Juliet' balcony. If you don't want to run to the expense of a balcony railing, a pane of 10 mm toughened glass fixed 1100 mm off the floor will keep you safe.

ROOFLIGHTS

Many of us have rooms where we have to switch on the lights during the grey days of winter, particularly in semi-detached and terraced houses where the windows are only at the front and back. There is only so much you can do to bring light into the centre of the home from two end walls, but you can look to the roof for light.

Light from above is better than light from the side. A rooflight, or skylight, that is half the size of a window will provide twice the light. Laid on the slope of your roof, a rooflight is likely to suffer from none of the shading obstructions that can bedevil a wall window, and since the light hits it more squarely, much more passes through.

The manufacturers of roof windows have targeted the loft-conversion market, and in doing so have developed their products for remedial installation rather than new build. For those of us looking to convert to greener homes, this is a happy coincidence. The windows are attractively priced, easy to fit into an existing roof and, to cap it all, have wooden frames rather than plastic. But why draw light into our lofts if we aren't converting them you may ask. The answer is that while letting daylight into your loft is still a good idea, getting it down into a room is even better, and this is the objective. Creating a light well between the ceiling and the

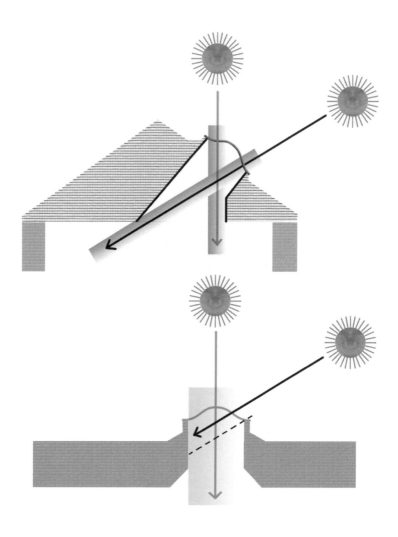

Penetration of light through rooflights on flat and sloping
roofs is enhanced by shaping the light well

rooflight isn't difficult in modern homes where the roof often has a shallow pitch.

Light wells are usually constructed from a timber framework that supports a plasterboard lining, and can also be insulated as necessary from the cold part of the attic. The rooflight and light well can be installed between the rafters and ceiling joists, or these can be cut back and the opening trimmed to allow a larger assembly to be fitted. Usually the trimming timbers are doubled around the opening

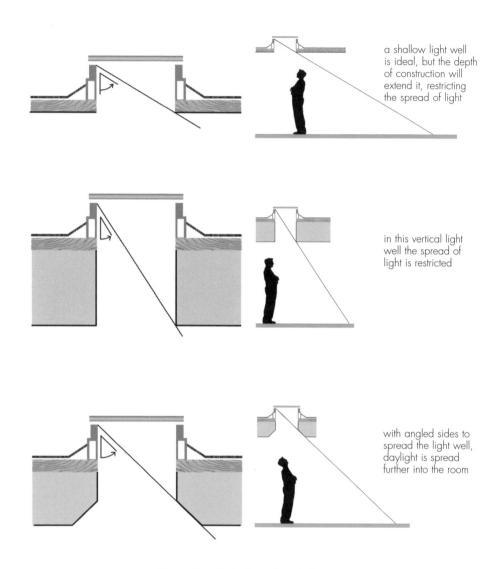

a shallow light well is ideal, but the depth of construction will extend it, restricting the spread of light

in this vertical light well the spread of light is restricted

with angled sides to spread the light well, daylight is spread further into the room

The angle of light through skylights

to support the cut rafters and joists, but since this is a structural alteration, you should take advice from a professional. Building codes and regulations usually apply to structural alterations like this.

If your roof is made from a series of trusses, under no circumstances should you cut them without obtaining an approved structural design. Trussed rafters comprise a web of thin timbers, joined by metal plates, which work in tension and compression, and they can't be cut and

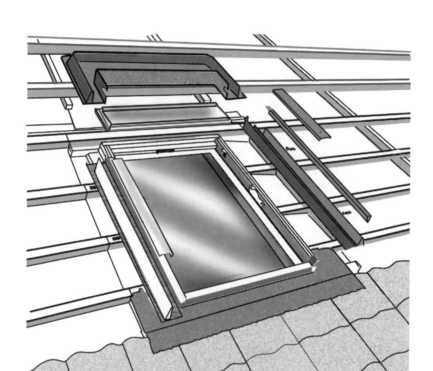

Kit form skylights are designed for easy installation

altered like a conventional 'cut-and-pitch' roof structure. Most trusses are set 600 mm apart, and slender rooflights are made to this width, which means that you won't need to cut through the sloping rafters or the ceiling ties.

Using 50 mm x 50 mm softwood and 9 mm plasterboard to form the shaft will keep the weight of the structure down to a level that the trusses should easily support, but if necessary bearers can spread the load over several of the ceiling ties.

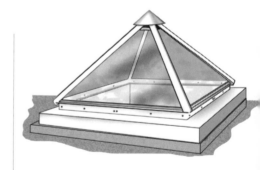

Pyramidal rooflight

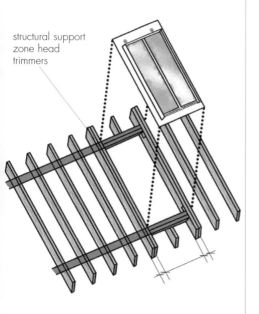

structural support
zone head
trimmers

Rooflight structure trimmings
around opening

Of course some of the light will be lost as it travels down the shaft, so it pays to keep it as short as you can, installing the roof window lower, rather than higher, on the roof. If the shaft ends up more than 1 m high, you will start to lose much of the light's brilliance. You can improve matters by painting the shaft white to reflect the daylight and splaying out the base as the ceiling joists allow to create a 'bell' shape that is wider at the bottom than the top. More than anything, a south-facing rooflight can bring a little sunshine into a dark part of your home, whether it's over the stairs or in a bedroom.

Channelling the light down even farther to the ground floor can be done, but it requires either a larger well or a shaft with a highly reflective surface. A larger light well will take up valuable floor space upstairs, so instead pipes made from shiny metal sheeting can

Conservation style rooflight

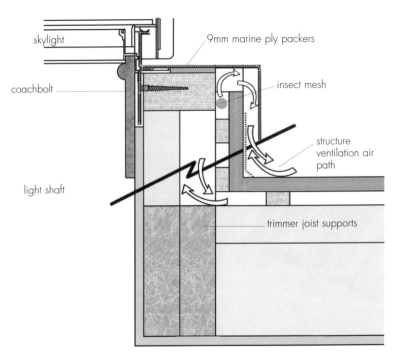

skylight

9mm marine ply packers

coachbolt

insect mesh

structure
ventilation air
path

light shaft

trimmer joist supports

Cross-section shows a ventilated roof cavity maintained around skylight

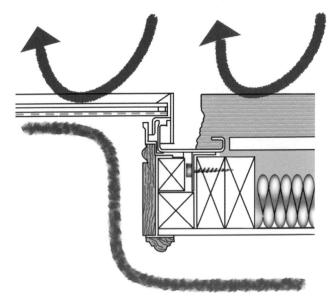

Cross-section shows a thermal break between skylight and roof

be used to create sunshine ducts, or light tubes, that beam the daylight down from the roof. In this case, the rooflight bit is little more than an acrylic dome or pyramid, while the pipes are only 300 mm or so in diameter, but they can be effective. The smaller ones have the benefit of fitting between floor joists and rafters without the need for cutting and trimming if you can get the alignment right, but they do tend to lose their effectiveness over a distance. I've planned to install a 300 mm diameter example, south-facing, that is about 3.6 m high from roof to ground-floor ceiling to boost the daylight in my kitchen, but I am aware that this is stretching its capabilities, and it may not prove as effective as I would like.

INSTALLING A LIGHT TUBE

Light tubes, or sun pipes, are a relatively new invention. They appeared in the early 1990s and have occupied a very tiny space in the market since then, not least because of their cost. Of the hundreds of building projects I become involved in each year, I only get to see a handful of these being installed; mostly they are in school corridors, which is a shame because they have the ability to effectively channel daylight into dark parts of our homes – daylight that keeps us from switching on light bulbs. In schools, where daytime use is predominant, the payback time on light tubes is thought to be as little as six years, but unfortunately in homes, you could look at 20 years as being more likely because they aren't very cheap to buy.

THE MAKE-UP OF LIGHT TUBES

Light tubes are little more than thin aluminium pipes that are pushed together in short sections to build a tube. The inner surface is highly polished and reflective, having either an anodized finish or a multi-layer polymeric film coating, which allows most of the daylight to bounce down the tube and into your room via a ceiling diffuser. Low technology to say the least, but they are effective. I have seen a 300 mm-diameter example, in bright sunshine, easily light a small internal bathroom. On dull and overcast days, the light level drops off rapidly, but for much of the time a tube of that size can light an area of 10 sq.m to a comfortable level. Some tubes look a bit like an aluminium version of the flexi-hose used for tumble driers and air vents, but although these are easier to install and are much cheaper, they don't have the reflective qualities necessary to make them worthwhile. When you realize that some reflection of light is knocked back at the roof lens, then again within the tube as it travels down it and finally at the diffuser, you can see that you can lose a good percentage of daylight in the equipment. Hence the shorter the tube and the wider its diameter, the more daylight you will receive. These tubes come in diameters up to 750 mm, but few of us can accommodate such a large duct in our homes. If all you had to run it through was the loft space, it might be possible, but for most lofts, a tube no more than 2 m long would allow a 300 mm-diameter model to be used quite satisfactorily.

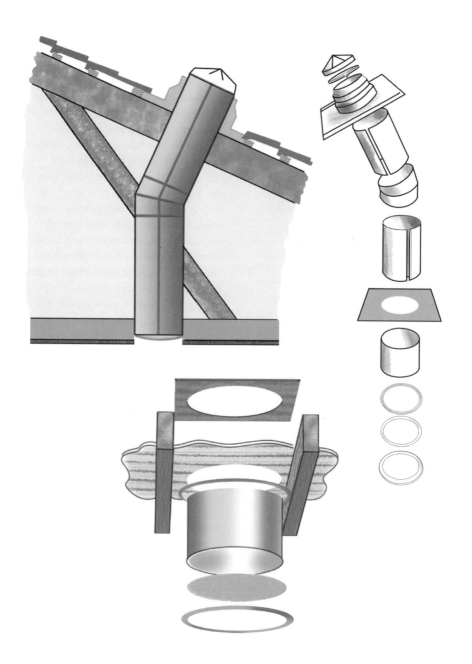

Light tubes are assembled from kits, in sections

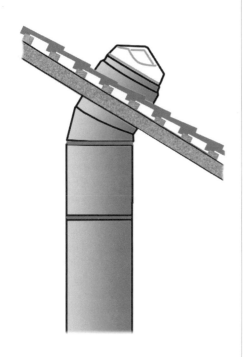

Assembled light tube

Converting to eco-friendly artificial light

Having done all you can to improve the natural light indoors, it is time to improve the artificial lighting. It is quite possible to save energy here by rethinking the way in which you light your home as well as changing to energy-efficient lamps.

As a rule, we tend to have a poor understanding of our lighting needs and often choose the wrong fittings. As a result, we end up wasting power with needlessly bright lighting and incorrect controls.

CONVERTING YOUR LIGHTING
In terms of conserving power, converting the lighting of your home to more eco-friendly status is the easiest way to achieve results.

Lighting tends to be forgotten until it is too late to reap the full benefits of choice and design, but with any eco-conversion project, it needs pushing to the front of your mind – well ahead of the decorating. Don't let your efforts stop at fitting a few low-energy light bulbs. You might also look at switching: an internal passive infra-red (PIR) switch (see Glossary page 169) or a programmable dimmer switch may be far more efficient than a manual switch that always produces full power and tends to be left on after the room has been vacated. Spaces that we visit temporarily are prone to this. Bathrooms, hallways, stairs and landings that we pass through are all ideal areas for automatic PIR detector switching.

Fitting a PIR that can be adjusted for the time period it stays on after the area has been vacated is essential. I have one that switches on a low-level brick light in my en-suite bathroom. It produces more than enough light from a 10 watt lamp to use the room at night without disturbing anyone and switches off a minute after the room has been left, just enough time to use the reflected light to find my way back to bed.

What matters most about lighting is getting it in the right place and achieving the right effect. Light can be stark and even, bright with contrasting shadow, soft and relaxing, and a variety of hues if not colours. Deciding on what you want for a particular room will mean thinking about how you plan to use that room. In

15

kitchens, adjustable and worktop lights should be employed as task lighting. Bathrooms, bedrooms and dining-rooms benefit from softer light to create a relaxed atmosphere, and lounges may need a variety of lighting options for reading, watching TV and so on. New homes often demonstrate an astounding lack of imagination when it comes to lighting, developers hanging a pendant fitting somewhere near the centre of each ceiling and leaving it at that. That is ambient or general lighting. It is the canvas on which you can create something better, something that is not only more energy-efficient, but also more imaginative and atmospheric. Eco-conversion work can give you the opportunity to install light fittings where you've always wanted them, to produce something unique, illuminating your home more effectively and efficiently to save energy in the process.

Energy-efficient lighting relies on three key elements:

- The right position

- The right light source

- The right light fitting

Position

Finding the right position for a light fitting might just be the hardest of the three. The lights in your home may not be in the best positions at present. Ceiling lights can be used for general lighting of a floor by placing them centrally, or as floodlights placed over a chair or sofa to pick out reading areas or work surfaces. Tungsten-filament pendant lights are often over-powered, 100 watts being common on a lounge ceiling, and this is a good place to start. A compact fluorescent lamp replacement of 11 watts will cope with the ambient lighting requirement in most lounges, providing the background (ambient) light source.

Not all of these lamps are pretty to look at, however, so you might consider fitting a shade beneath it to deflect the light up and across the ceiling. If you do, make sure it is highly reflective because you will lose brightness in the reflection. Swirl and decor bulb shapes are available if they will be visible.

In most cases, the right position for a light must ensure that the sharp glare from the lamp itself doesn't hit us in the eyes. With spots and LEDs (light emitting diodes), if the lamps themselves can't be seen, just the light from them, then that is good positioning. If you've ever had a glass table lamp, you'll know what I mean. The glare of the bulb fills your retina, even when you aren't looking at it. In the early 1980s, fluorescent strip lights with their stark illumination were often fitted in kitchens where strong lighting is needed. They do cast a shadowless, even light over everything when mounted to a ceiling, but the fitting might take the older-style tubes known as T12s; T8s are the energy-efficient replacements for these, and apart from being slightly thinner, they appear no different. They are, however, classed in the energy-efficient category.

Reading lights are a form of task light, but it isn't always easy to direct them. You might prefer the freedom of being able to move furniture like armchairs and study desks around, in which case you won't want to fix a wall or ceiling light in any position. Portable plug-in lamps are the answer, but they may only use tungsten-halogen bulbs, so make sure they come with dimmer controls. I have a portable standard lamp that combines an uplighter and a smaller reading light on a flexible stalk, both of which are dimmable, but I'd be even happier if the reading light was an LED cluster.

Light source
ENERGY-SAVING LAMPS
Just by changing two filament light bulbs for compact fluorescent ones, you can save the equivalent of 1 tonne of coal from the fire over its lifetime. I'm sure Edison would approve. It was a neat idea of his to heat up a thin wire filament in a glass bulb until it glowed white hot, but really it is time for a change.

Ironically we are going back to gas lights long after Edison got us away from them – compact fluorescent lamps (CFLs) work by using electricity to agitate gas molecules, which then emit light. In this way, the standard CFL bulb burns for 8000 hours, emitting a warm white light with a colour temperature of around the 2700 k mark. This soft light can be misinterpreted as being 'dim', even though a 25 watt CFL will produce around 1600 lumens (comparable to the strengh of a 100 watt tungsten filament bulb).

The reason for this is the low temperature of the light. We have developed a taste for a cleaner, whiter light, more akin to daylight. I strongly believe that it has been the light temperature that has put many people off replacing their tungsten-filament bulbs with energy-efficient ones. That combined

with a restricted availability of compatible decorative fittings, and the fact that you couldn't use any controls with them beyond a rocker switch. They haven't been compatible with dimmers and automatic sensors, but recently some manufacturers have cracked those nuts.

Daylight-simulation CFLs are now available with a colour temperature between 5000 and 6350 k, similar to daylight with that cooler, bright bluish white light we've enjoyed with halogens. If you want to replace some power draining spotlights in the kitchen for

---

UNITS OF LIGHT

Lumen (lm) – luminous power (or lux)

Luminosity or Luminance – the emission or reflectance of light

Efficacy – measured as lumens per watt (lm/k); theoretical maximum of 683, but should be at least 40 for energy efficiency (eg. 30 lumens from 18 white LEDs of 180mA consumption – 10 mA per bulb)

Candela (cd) – unit of luminous intensity

Lux (lx) – Unit of illumination on a surface (lumen per square metre)

Power – consumption in milliamps (mA)

Watts (W) – power output: approximately 1 watt creates 10 lumens

---

LEDs are good for task (reading) lighting when they can be focused close to the subject in a narrow beam (eg. 20–30 degrees).

Different styles for energy efficient lamps

TYPICAL COMPACT FLUORESCENT LAMP PERFORMANCE			
CFL	**TFL equivalent**	**Lumens**	**Life (hrs)**
7 watts	30 watts	220	8000
9 watts	40 watts	450	8000
13 watts	60 watts	800	8000
18 watts	75 watts	1100	8000
25 watts	100 watts	1600	10,000

example, you can now find floodlight reflectors in the daylight group that are still energy-efficient bulbs of up to 40 watts. At this end, they would be equal to 75 watts in a tungsten-filament floodlight. That is the top end, brightness-wise; you could come down to 20 watt reflectors if they were carefully directed to reduce your power consumption.

These floodlights aren't as efficient as standard CFLs, however, as you can see from the accompanying table. You can interpret 'lumens' as brightness.

The warm and softer light of 13 watt CFLs can be used in bedrooms and dining-rooms where subdued lighting is agreeable. You can find them in decor globe format or swirled into artistic tubular corkscrews, capable of being fitted to a range of light fittings, although not all. Replacing your bedroom ceiling lamps with CFLs is the ideal place to start. For reading and in bathrooms, where a cooler light might be better, look for those CFLs with a colour temperature of around 4100 k – not quite daylight, but close.

Controls have been the other big stumbling block with these lamps. We need dimmable lights in most of our reception rooms and bedrooms today, allowing us to adjust the lumen output to suit our mood. At long last, some CFLs are now compatible with dimmer controls where the light can be reduced down to around 20 per cent of its full brightness. They aren't common yet, and you will have to seek them out from specialist suppliers. It is also possible to use them with PIR motion detectors and photoelectric switches that operate at dusk, which means that at last we can have our garden security lights saving energy and money for us rather than burning electricity.

LIGHT EMITTING DIODES (LEDS)

An exciting discovery has been made in recent years with those little red diodes that started life in the 1960s in calculator displays. Somebody found a way of making them white, improving their brightness and clustering them into useful lamps. We've had coloured light emitting diodes for decades, but white had long been a problem. This was solved by surrounding a blue LED with a

A GU10 fitting (left) can house a cluster of tiny LEDs (enlarged, right)

phosphorescent dye that glows white when the blue light hits it. Fluorescent lamps employ a very similar trick by producing ultra-violet light in the tube and using a glass coating to turn it white. The technology is improving all the time.

LEDs may give a clean white light, but individually it is not very bright. Consequently to light a room with them effectively, they have to be clustered into substantial groups. A cluster might comprise 20 LEDs, all neatly packed into a circular lamp like a GU10 fitting, commonly used for recessed halogen spot lamps. A light fitting like this would normally have housed a low-voltage or mains halogen lamp of 35 or maybe 50 watts. Bright, white and hot – very hot. In

this same size fitting, 20 LEDs will glow using just 2 watts altogether, 0.1 watt (100 mW) each. Not only will they do this, but also they will do it without giving off any heat. I have held my hand almost touching one and there was not a suspicion of heat coming off it. The room I was in was a loft-conversion bedroom with a low ceiling, and the halogen lamps that had been installed in every other loft conversion and extension I'd visited would have heated a similar room to an uncomfortable level.

Halogens were designed as spot lamps, and recessing them into ceilings, as so many of us have been doing since the 1990s, meant that they focused bright shafts of light on to the surface below. If that surface was the floor, the ceiling had to have quite a few lamps dotted over it to light the whole room. These lights are ideal for task lighting where you need bright and directed light, but they rarely get used for that. Instead we have peppered our ceilings with them to create ambient light the hard way, and in so doing have wasted a lot of power and created a lot of unwanted heat. In a low ceiling where your head is not far beneath the lights, feeling the scorch of halogen every time you walk beneath one is unpleasant. In one standard sized kitchen, I counted 20 halogen spots in the ceiling, each burning 35 watts – that's 700 watts at the flick of a switch, and almost enough residual heat to make toast.

LEDs run cold, making them perfect for low ceilings. There is something you should know, however – the actual light they give off (measured in candles) is low, so if you plan to use them for ambient lighting, you will need an awful lot to achieve the desired light level. At only 2500 mcd (1000 mcd = 1 candela) per bulb, you'll need 2 LEDs to equal the power of five candles. We won't be using them in lighthouses, but I'm sure that in the future advances will be made to increase their output, and when it

CHANGING LOW-VOLTAGE HALOGENS FOR LEDS

Note that 12 volt (extra-low-voltage) LEDs will not tolerate voltage swings created by wire-wound ballasted transformers. Electronic LED-compatible transformers are required if you're planning to replace your 12 volt halogen lamps with 12 volt LEDs.

LED light with remote transformer

does, they may take over from tubular fluorescent lamps as the standard low-energy light.

An average sized double bedroom might have a dozen fittings in the ceiling, each covering 1 sq.m of floor with light. Rooms like bedrooms, dining-rooms and landings, where softer light levels are ideal, are most suited to them. Lounges, kitchens and reception rooms tend to need

LED LIFE

LEDs have a life expectancy of around 30,000 hours, which, according to my pocket calculator, means that you could leave them switched on for 24 hours a day, every day for almost four years before they needed to be replaced. Effectively, in normal use, you can forget about having to change them.

21

brighter ambient lights or task lighting, so I would avoid them in such situations.

LED EFFICIENCY

Power consumption runs with brightness, and energy efficiency measures brightness in lumens per circuit watt of power. Typically 18 white LED bulbs in a fitting might produce 30 lumens of light for 180 mA of current, about 1.3 watts of power. This amounts to about 70 mW per bulb. Coloured LEDs offer a lower lumen output – around 20 in the same fitting.

The measure for energy efficiency to kick in has been set at the around the 40 lumens per circuit watt mark. Given this specification, they fall short, but I'm sure their performance will be improved in the near future, so keep an eye on the data. At present, they need using in the right place, and that is where we all could sort out our light energy use. Wasted light is wasted power and money. Directing light where it is needed, in the right levels, is far more important than covering your home in 40 lumens per circuit watt.

In a nutshell, LEDs aren't much more efficient than tungsten-filament bulbs at present in this context, which is why you can't afford to use them to illuminate rooms with ambient light and expect to save energy.

CABINET AND WORKTOP LIGHTING WITH LEDS

We tend to go for decorative lighting of cabinets these days, as well as functional under-unit lighting of worktops. Both are ideal tasks for LEDs, which can be installed as clusters in GU10 fittings or slotted individually into tiny drilled holes. The angle of light reflectance is worth

Flush mounted fittings

noting in these situations. It is as variable with LEDs as it is with other lamps. A 30-degree angle would be defined as narrow, for spotlighting purposes, and a 130-degree angle would be defined as broad for wide-angle light. This is particularly important with LEDs because brightness is proportional to beam angle. A narrow beam will be much brighter than a spread one. For example, seven bulbs focused on a 20-degree spread will achieve the same lumens as 48 spread over a 50-degree beam. Forgetting the science, one cluster of 20 LEDs in a GU10, spaced at 600 mm intervals above a worktop will work brilliantly to light it from beneath wall cupboards or a pelmet.

ELECTROLUMINESCENT LIGHTING

Don't get too excited if you haven't heard of this. It is a new form of cool burning, energy-efficient lighting that, at present, is really only usable in signage and decor. A tiny capacitor is printed on a silkscreen with a phosphorous-based ink on its surface. When a small electrical field passes over the capacitor, it excites the ink's electrons and illuminates them. These are sometimes referred to as light emitting capacitors (LECs).

LECs are wafer thin and flexible, and can be adhered to almost any surface, but to date you might be most familiar with them in the display of your mobile phone or car dashboard. For safety marker lights on stairs, they could be ideal, but most of the advances in this material seem to be in the glowing, colour splashed world of advertising, where it is being employed with great creativity. I suspect that LECs will become available for installation in our homes to enhance the decor in a room, rather than illuminate it.

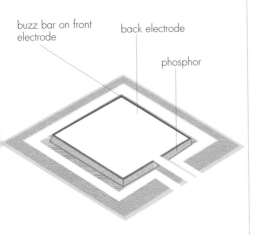

buzz bar on front electrode

back electrode

phosphor

Electroluminescent cell structure

THE COLOUR OF LIGHT

Lamps are a long way from being white all the time, but then white is not always the colour you want. Apart from the many coloured lamps available, which tend to provide significantly lower illumination, specific types of lamp have unique hues, determined by their colour temperature.

The varying wavelengths in light's electromagnetic spectrum are interpreted by our brains as colours – red for the longest wavelengths (700 mn) and lowest frequencies, violet at the shortest wavelengths (400 mn) and highest frequencies. The colours of the rainbow fall between them. Outside of those limits, our eyes can't see the infra-red before the red kicks in, or the ultra-violet after the violet drops out. We can, however, feel the heat from infra-red light on our skin. The lower the colour temperature, the warmer the light. Take candle light for example. At less than 2000 deg.k, it is edging out of the red and into the orange end of the spectrum. Sunlight on a summer's day is in the middle of the scale at around 5500 deg.k, but rising up into a blue sky away from sunlight sees the colour temperature increase to 9000 deg.k.

Light fittings

Without the right fitting, your choice of light source and position will have been wasted. The fitting determines how the light is directed around it and reflects the architecture of your home and its interior design. Choosing the right shade will also affect the light level. One fitting you can easily change is the living-room light switch; swapping it for a dimmer switch will give you the chance of altering the ambient (or background) light level.

23

A COMPARISON OF FIVE LAMP TYPES

TUNGSTEN-FILAMENT

Energy efficiency variable between 1 and 20 lumens per watt, but generally very poor with an average inefficiency of 91 per cent. The traditional standard bulb has a yellowish light of 2000 deg.k. unless in a corrective blue glass bulb as a daylight correction type. This type of lamp should not be used for ambient lighting due to its power consumption and short life expectancy.

TUNGSTEN-HALOGEN

Very popular since the 1990s. White and crisp light, typical as low-voltage or mains-voltage recessed spotlights. Colour temperature of around 3000 deg.k. Small and long lasting, tungsten-halogen lamps produce focused light that works well in uplighters and downlighters. The low-voltage types do have slightly better energy efficiency, but the transformers needed to convert mains-voltage to low-voltage use power inefficiently and thus are a problem. As small spotlights, they should not be used in multiples to provide ambient lighting.

METAL-HALIDE

New for domestic interior use, these lamps offer high efficiency, making them cheap to run. In the form of high-intensity-discharge (HID), they have been used in car headlamps and street lighting as sodium (orange glow) lamps – the most efficient light source known to man. Now also in garden spotlights. For indoor use, the white light halides have five times the efficiency of standard tungsten bulbs. In this form, they provide the most natural light available at between 4200 and 4600 deg.k.

FLUORESCENT

TUBULAR: The light tends to be cold and bluish from standard fluorescents, but the new types (T8s) are far more energy-efficient than the previous T12s. Diffusers help kill the glare, but look cheap and collect flies, making them undesirable.

COMPACT: Daylight versions are ideal for ambient lighting of rooms and as spotlights. Usually they give off a warmer light. They are highly energy-efficient and last eight times longer than tungsten-filament lamps.

LEDS

The energy efficiency of these – 15–20 lumens per watt at present – is considered poor, but is likely to increase with advances in technology. The temperature of white LEDs is very close to daylight, with a slightly blue cast, making them an ideal pure light source for task and accent lighting.

The art of lighting

Now that we have the three ingredients for lighting, how do we use them to best effect? You can split lighting effects into five distinct techniques:

AMBIENT (BACKGROUND)

The general light reflected across a room to provide constant, level illumination that is functional, but featureless and free from shadows, is the ambient light. Outdoors the ambient light would be filtered through clouds on a sunless day to be cast uniformly and evenly on the ground. Indoors the standard ceiling pendant lamp gives ambient light when dressed with a lampshade. Ambient light should always be dimmable.

ACCENT

Because ambient light flattens everything, accent light is needed to highlight shapes and textures. You can pick out architectural features, like an alcove or a fireplace, or objects such as pictures or treasured ornaments. The only exception would be furniture: lighting a chair will draw unwanted attention to a recumbent family member, while on a table or work surface, it becomes task lighting. Accent lighting is valuable in most rooms, but it is particularly beneficial in reception rooms. Spotlights, table lamps and picture lights can all be used as accent lighting, depending on how you want a feature to be displayed. Note that these can amount to a significant energy loss if you employ tungsten-halogen spots! At last, however, we can use something that will generate light that is just as pure and white, but consume a fraction of the power – LEDs. They are the perfect accent lights.

TASK

Task lighting is what you get from lighting a chair or a worktop. It sounds like it should only be employed in the kitchen or in a study, but when you think about it, there are tasks of some kind or another to do in all rooms, and being able to see well to carry out those tasks is important. Task lighting needs to be bright and targeted so that it is restricted to a particular area and doesn't spill out elsewhere. Reflective shading can be used to achieve this, but it wastes the energy consumed by the light. It is far better if the light is directional. An example of this would be study desk lamps. Being low and shaded, they cast the light down on to the desktop without it spilling around the room or up into your eyes.

DECORATIVE

Lighting for decorative purposes should not to be ignored. Whether it be the sparkle of a glass chandelier or colour from halogen lamps splashed across a wall, decorative lighting is an extension of interior decoration that complements the paint and fabrics.

If you've seen home makeover programmes on TV, the only LEDs you might be familiar with are the micro star type that sit inside a rubber grommet. These tiny lights can be fixed (with the grommet acting as the nut) to any surface to create something individual. They are extremely flexible. With any kind of light, you should place it or shade it to prevent it from shining directly into your eyes. LEDs can be fitted into floors as uplights, but if you do this they really can only be installed around the perimeter so that they illuminate the wall. Anything else will be irritating for your eyes, if not retina damaging. Although not quite as damaging as laser beams, they are very intense light sources and you should never look directly into them.

For decorative light to work well, the level of ambient light in the room should be low, enabling it to be seen to its best effect. Fibre-optic lights are available for creating your own starlit night on room surfaces, and LECs and LEDs are the only eco-friendly solutions.

CANDLELIGHT

Firelight and candlelight are the most natural forms of 'artificial' lighting. The dancing flames of a fire or the flicker and glow of a candle bring a special quality that is impossible to replicate with lamps. With firelight, it's the campfire security thing that reassures us that we are safe from the creatures of the night, and with candlelight it's the romantic glow that reassures us that we may not be safe from the creatures of the night!

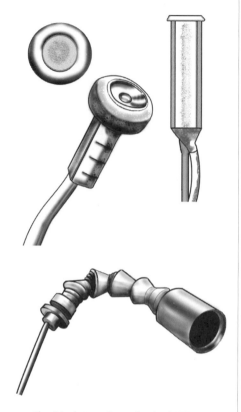

Flexible fittings for individual LEDs

We have grown a little unfamiliar with the risks of using fire for light, however, and candles, oil burners and real fires need care and attention if they aren't to lead to accidents. Naked flames need positioning carefully and treating with some respect, so give some thought to what may be above a candle or an oil burner before you light it – a wooden shelf, a curtain? They may seem out of reach, but the heat alone from the flame could blacken them or, worse, ignite them, even without its touch.

The amount of light

Because most of us have not given much, if any, thought to how much light we need and its cost to the world, we have been over-lighting our homes. It isn't easy to estimate how much light you need until you've spent some time turning down lights or switching them off because they annoy you. You might want to experiment with an extension cable and various lamps to see just how much light each can generate. Not only will this give you ideas of the type of lamp you'll need, but also its wattage, or power. The only problem is that it will be difficult to visualize the final effect until the decorating is complete.

White walls reflect about 70 per cent of the light falling on them; dark ones may return only 30 per cent; grey slate floors will absorb all but ten per cent of the light shining on them. As a rough guide, dining-rooms need about 50 lux (soft enough to produce a relaxed atmosphere, but sufficient to be able to see what you're eating), kitchens should have about 300 lux, as should stairways for safety. The spread of light is also an issue, and for this you need to be aware of the angle of the beam generated by a particular lamp. The packaging should reveal this. Those halogen spots we peppered our ceilings with in the late 1990s burned 35 or 50 watts of power each, but they only shed about 500 lux to the floor directly beneath them. With a low-angle beam, they don't spread light very far.

Lamps and heat

Heat has been an unfortunate by-product of many modern lamps. Halogen and dichroic reflector lamps produce a lot of it and must be placed at a suitable

26

distance from their subject. Dichroics throw the heat back through the glass and shouldn't be fitted in ceilings without fireproof covers. These small hoods prevent the heat from being transferred to the structure and charring it. They also act to 'repair' the hole in the fire-resistant ceiling. In the USA, uplighters with halogen lamps in them gave rise to so many house fires that it soon became a requirement for manufacturers to fit protectors over them. As plug-in floorstand lights, they might house 300 watt halogens that get a little hot. LEDs are the only lights that run cold, but you will need to cluster at least 200 of them (totalling 20 watts) in a fitting to achieve an ambient uplighter.

Outdoor lighting

Making our gardens eco-friendly is not just about conserving water; conserving power in them has never been easier. Garden lighting needs to be just as carefully planned as lighting indoors, so that the best features are revealed. Accent lighting using solar energy is an effective way to achieve this, but you will need to keep the lights low and fairly close to the subject. This should help to prevent light from spilling into other parts of the garden or your neighbours' gardens and generally becoming a nuisance. Uplighting will be easier to achieve with low-energy spotlights of 20 watts, but sometimes even they will need a baffle or a shield of some kind to prevent the light from oversailing the object you are aiming it at. You can reduce the amount of spread laterally by choosing spots over floods, or by placing a tube (such as a short piece of drainpipe) over a ground lamp to baffle it.

Light pollution has left us living beneath an iridescent glow that covers the night sky, blanking out the stars. Starlight travels a long way to reach us, and it seems sad that after a journey of hundreds, if not thousands, of years, we blank it out in the last few seconds.

It became common to use 500 watt halogen floodlights on the walls of our homes with PIR detectors that scan half the garden and the adjacent pavement for movement. Besides the vast power drain they created, these lights did nothing to improve any home, and they have even been said to reduce security by providing too much glare. Think about it. Our pupils enlarge in the dark to see better and contract when they encounter bright light, which means that we see less in the dark shadows outside the pool of light. A 20 or 40 watt energy-efficient spotlight lamp, such as those in the compact fluorescent range, is just as effective when positioned correctly. You can use them closer to the area you want to light and control the detection zone more tightly. To reduce glare, the angle of the beam should be below 70 degrees anyway, but the nearer to vertical it is, the better.

Garden candles and solar powered table lamps are ideal if you have the room for them when you're eating. Better still are the lights that can be clipped to the underside of a parasol.

You can use daylight sensors to switch on the lights at night, but they will remain on throughout the hours of darkness, so it is better to use a PIR detector to automatically switch the lighting on and off at times when it can be appreciated. There is no benefit in having outside lights turned on all the time.

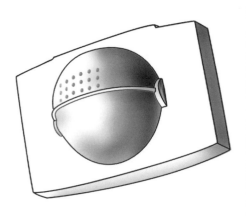

Internal PIR detector

With solar powered lights, at least there is no cost to having them on until the battery runs out, so it is worth looking for unique and interesting features in your garden to illuminate as well as the edges of pathways and drives. Look for shape and texture over colour, which beyond green will appear less than colourful under artificial light. What you really need is a striking subject with some structure to it. Plants described as 'architectural' are perfect.

SOLAR POWERED LEDS

The versatility of LEDs in fittings and locations means that they can be encased in stainless steel or brass, or waterproofed in plastic and made entirely submersible. You can light ponds, fountains and waterfalls creatively with LEDs, but even more importantly, you can run them for free with solar power. LEDs are perfect for solar powered lighting because they last

for so long: they can be fitted in sealed units that are weathertight, in the knowledge that the lamps will never need to be changed. Marker lights are commonly available with solar panels (the amorphous-film type) incorporated in the lamp cover. These are ideal for defining the edges of a garden path or pond. They can be incredibly cheap (particularly those made in the Far East), although I've seen plenty where the solar panel has flaked off due to the low quality of manufacture.

Security lamps that cast sufficient light across a dark corner or a doorway can be fitted with both a solar panel to power them and the usual PIR motion sensor to activate them. Because the LEDs consume such a tiny amount of electricity, the solar panel can charge up a replaceable lead-acid battery with enough electricity to run a light for a month or two. If the sun disappears for a couple of weeks, the light won't stop working.

The light levels in security lights need some consideration. Those 500 watt floodlights can't be replaced with LEDs, nor indeed can the smaller 150 watt mini-floodlights. In this respect, you are looking at a lamp of, say, 20 LEDs being equal to a 7 watt compact fluorescent or a 20 watt halogen. Door or sign illumination would be a more suitable use for them. There are LEDs of 1 watt bulb power, and four of these would do the job of ten times that number in the usual 5 mm (0.1 watt) size. Installed in a mini-flood fitting, they would be equal to 60 watts with about 650 lumens. This is more likely to meet ground illuminating security needs with the help of the silver reflective fitting.

The solar panels can be quite small.

One measuring 225 mm x 150 mm by 18 mm thick makes a 17 volt panel about the size of a thin brick, which is enough to power a 1 watt LED lamp.

I've often used brick lights for illuminating outdoor steps and driveway entrances. As they come in brick size to discourage vandalism and prevent accidental damage, they can be built flush into walls, with only the lens glass and the bulb behind it left vulnerable. With LEDs, the lamps can be encased in a solid brick of acrylic, making them entirely damage resistant. An LED brick might contain around 36 bulbs, although these are often 12 volt direct-current models, which means connecting them to a suitable transformer. Mini-brick LED lights are available as well, but since they are too small to replace a standard brick, they can only be installed with extra building work to make good around them. I am at a loss to explain why they are made to that size; brick lights have always been brick sized!

Safety lighting

Small children and half-awake adults are prone to doing a lot of damage at night.

Either to the electricity bill by switching on all the lights when they get up for the bathroom or a drink and forgetting to switch them off when they go back to bed, or to themselves by stumbling. What would help would be some low-level marker lights that use little electricity and act like runway lights on an airfield to guide them safely about the home.

If you plan on lighting a stairway for night-time safety, LECs and LEDs are ideal. Located in the strings (sides of the stairs) or the risers (vertical parts of the stairs), they can produce enough light to illuminate the stair treads. LEDs fitted in 50 mm diameter saucers may comprise small clusters of perhaps only three bulbs, but these will be enough to find your way safely on a staircase at night without waking the whole house. A PIR sensor can be employed to switch them on at the top and bottom of a flight.

Do remember that an indoor PIR also needs a daylight sensor if it is to function only when the light levels are low enough for lighting to be necessary. You don't want it switching on the lights when there is enough daylight not to need them.

CHAPTER TWO

Power

We no longer have to draw all of our electricity from a grid at the mercy of power companies and at the cost of depleting fossil fuels like coal and natural gas. Technology in the 21st century has brought us the opportunity of living off-grid for at least part of the time, with some of our power harvested from nature – from the energy of the sun and wind, and the growth of plants. In the past, self-sufficiency meant growing your own food, but things are changing – now it also means producing your own energy. Harvesting the power in nature and converting your home to become its own power station offers the prospect of living off-grid, unaffected by politics and global conglomerates, able to use as much energy as you want and for free. A life without fuel bills sounds like liberation to me, but how easy is it to achieve?

The solution to reducing carbon emissions has been obvious for so long it's been embarrassing. What's been holding us back is primarily the cost of alternative energy. Converting your home into an independent power station isn't cheap, but technology is advancing all the time and soon it will be much more affordable. We have to bear in mind that if we all contribute a bit, the global effect will make it worthwhile and that, at the beginning of the 21st century, we are still at the dawn of alternative energy technology, much of which until now has only been used in the space programme. It will become better, cheaper and more available, and all of us will be able to do something to create our own electricity and enjoy self-sufficiency – at least in part.

Our need for power

Even environmentalists will tell you that becoming entirely independent for all your electricity needs is difficult to say the least; impossible would be nearer the truth at the moment, due almost entirely to the way we live. There are technologies available for capturing the energy of the sun and the wind, and converting it into electricity, but all generate an intermittent supply, and to live from them alone would mean enduring hardships that most of us wouldn't care to contemplate. So they exist as options for a secondary supply. When installed, however, they become the primary source of power, which means that only when they can't be employed does your power supply switch automatically to the national grid. In every other sense, they are secondary sources of energy because the power they generate will be significantly less over the year than that received from the grid, but that shouldn't put anyone off.

Since Edison invented the light bulb, we have changed our nature so that we require less sleep, extending our days into the nights and using power in every minute of every day.

The natural rhythm of day and night meant that our body clocks were programmed to need an absolute minimum of eight-and-a-half hours of sleep if we were to function properly, but artificial light changed that, while our needs grew to accomplish more. Now sleeping is often thought of as a waste of time. You might be switching off the light when you go to bed, but your TV may be sleeping on stand-by, your dishwasher

THE POWER OF APPLIANCES

	Consumption (watts/hr)	Input (watts)
Fast-boil kettle		3000
Microwave oven		800
Cooker	1000	
Iron		1500
Dishwasher	800	
Fridge/freezer		2250
Tumble dryer	4000	
Washing machine	1000	
Hairdryer		2000
Vacuum cleaner		2000
Shower		10,500
Radiator		3000

NOTE: Large appliances are rated by consumption of electricity (watts/hr), while smaller appliances are rated by their input (watts).

timed to begin the nightshift, while outside the street lamps are burning. Our power needs ebb and flow, but the need is always there. Peak demands occur around noon and early evening, but we never stop wanting electricity, even when we are asleep.

Indeed our demand for it has grown massively, partly because it allows us to save time, and time has been extensively crushed into our lives today. It's said that microwave ovens only save us four minutes of time a day. Yet most people use one because those four minutes are crucial to them. Microwaves use anything between 700 and 900 watts, albeit briefly.

Even electric kettles are becoming increasingly power thirsty to achieve a faster boiling time, because we can't wait that extra minute to make a cup of tea. With most appliances, it isn't easy to find

out how much of a thirst for power they have; you normally won't find it in the user guide, so you might have to try a bit harder and search the product itself for a label. The table above will give you an idea of what most electrical appliances burn, but if you want to check yourself, you can buy a cheap plug-in energy meter that will record the amount of power any appliance uses when plugged in to it. Some will store the information on a number of appliances, so you can move it around the home looking for the worst offenders.

Then, of course, we have our lights – a kilowatt or two there is easily achieved. It all adds up to a few thousand kilowatt/hrs every year for the average home. Worldwide it adds up to 320 billion kilowatt/hrs a year – the energy demand of the earth's population. As a result, our homes' need for electricity causes more carbon to be released into the atmosphere than is generated by our cars, yet we tend to think of the latter as the world's biggest polluters. Most modest European homes effectively produce 6 tonnes of carbon, enough to fill six giant hot-air balloons purely with carbon dioxide.

Solar power

So where are we going to find that kind of energy without burning coal or gas, or mucking around with nuclear isotopes? The answer is that it finds us. The sun isn't expected to die for some time yet, and every hour of every day it delivers enough energy to meet the whole world's demands for two years. That energy comes in the form of light and it takes roughly eight minutes to make the 93 million mile journey to your roof. In fact, even in a cloudy temperate region like British Columbia, you could still expect to find 1000 kilowatt/hrs of solar radiation bouncing off every square metre of south-facing roof (in the northern hemisphere) every year; in a southerly desert region like Mexico, you could more than double that. It means that, in theory, we could all meet our power needs with solar radiation if only we could harness it. Sadly we are only just beginning to find a way of doing that, and the best we can do at present is to capture about 15 per cent of it. That small amount can be caught by the relatively new technology of photo-voltaic cells.

PHOTO-VOLTAIC SYSTEMS

Using solar power to generate electricity, rather than simply heat water, is now possible thanks to the relatively new

technology of photo-voltaic (PV) cells. These are the blue-grey glassy panels you see on some roadside equipment and some garden lights. They are made of silicon cells protected by glass. Photo-voltaics were developed by NASA (the USA's National Aeronautics and Space Administration) so that its satellites and spacecraft could power themselves using solar radiation; indeed their effectiveness is closely linked to solar irradiation. To put it simply – the more sunlight falling on them, the more effective they are and so, although they still work shaded or beneath cloudy skies, they work better when exposed to the sun. Output increases with direct radiation (sunlight) and reduces with diffused radiation (cloudy conditions).

There are three main types of PV panel: monocrystalline, polycrystalline (also known as multicrystalline) and amorphous thin film. The last is the lightest, most flexible and, strangely enough, most efficient in cloudy conditions, but the monocrystalline type is the best overall and is used for most

PV CELL TYPES AND PERFORMANCE CELL EFFICIENCY (%)	
Thin-film (amorphous) silicon	5
Polycrystalline silicon	12–15
Monocrystalline silicon	13–17

These figures don't look very impressive until you appreciate that the conversion of fossil fuels into electricity isn't efficient either. It averages 30 per cent – not very efficient and environmentally destructive into the bargain.

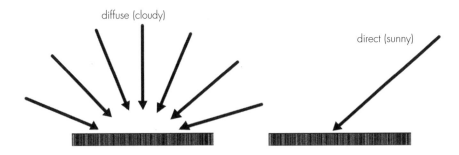

diffuse (cloudy)

direct (sunny)

UV radiation arrives, both with diffused light on cloudy days and direct sunlight on clear days

domestic PV systems. Efficiency means you need less in terms of area, and since the roof of your home is a finite space, it is the preferred type. Generating power in this way is only possible on a highly localized scale, on a house by house basis. If home developers had to install community PV arrays to power their new houses, the land requirement would be too great for many countries to bear. In the UK, for example, where over 30,000 PV panels would serve at best 1800 homes and cover a small field, this would not be an option. Indeed the space requirement of a PV panel power station is judged to be about 37 times greater than a nuclear power station.

Solar panels need space, and at present it is best if the space already exists. As it happens, it does – on the roofs and walls of buildings.

In most of Europe, crystalline cells prevail, but because of the preponderance of lightweight roof shingles in the USA, flexible amorphous-film cells are more common. At present all are made from silicon and are expensive. Unfortunately they are too expensive to make them prolific, and they are only being installed

where government grants are being given as incentives. The research being done into new cells is directed toward finding a replacement material for silicon that is inexpensive and just as efficient, and the ultra-lightweight amorphous-film type seems to offer the most promise in this respect. If a new and efficient method of producing thin-film cells is found, it would dramatically reduce the cost of photo-voltaic solar panels, and silicon would become the Betamax format of the solar energy world.

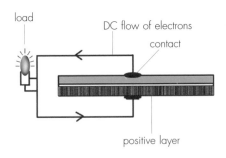

load

DC flow of electrons

contact

positive layer

PV cell

HOW THEY WORK

Silicon is used for PV cells because it has the ability not only to capture the photons in sunlight, but also to dislodge the outer electrons of their atoms and push them along to the next atom, thus creating a chain of moving electrons. With these electrons on the march, all it needs is a wire attached to them and they will march down it to supply an electric current. If this seems an over-simplified version of the technology, I apologize, but it is the only one that I can begin to understand. Apparently it takes an awful lot of electrons to shift along before a usable current is produced. Take a domestic lighting circuit, for example, running on the usual 5 amps of circuit current. To achieve that flow, no fewer than 30 million million million electrons have to be moved per second. Thankfully electrons are so small and so easily moved by this process that this is entirely achievable. Each cell has two layers of silicon, one with a positive charge, the other with a negative charge to keep the electrons flowing between them under the bombardment of solar energy.

Electricity generated in this fashion flows in one direction only, which means it is direct current (DC) and not alternating current (AC), as used in homes in the UK. With alternating current, the electrons head off in the opposite direction about 50 times every second. For those who need AC power, there are three possible solutions to the problem. Firstly direct current can be stored in batteries to power 12 volt appliances, and you could convert all your household equipment to rechargeable 12 volt types, although this is not really an option.

Secondly you can use batteries and an inverter to convert 12 volts DC into 240 volts AC, or thirdly you could opt for the most popular solution, which is to connect your solar panels to the national grid and redirect any surplus electricity back to it once the batteries are fully charged. The last is known as a grid-support system and incorporates a meter that measures how much electricity is sent to the grid. This produces an income from the electricity supplier.

It sounds good doesn't it? Reversing the role by sending your electricity company a quarterly bill. With all the renewable power sources, however, the most effective gains are made by using the power in the building where it has been generated. Although some of the power can be stored in batteries, this does not amount to much, and it would be impossible to house enough of them to service all your power needs. As a result, you are always going to have electricity you can't use and frequently you will have electricity demands that your solar system can't meet – simply because you may want to watch TV after sunset or something equally inconvenient.

Solar generated electricity is available intermittently, and the level of access to it depends on nature and geography. If you are fortunate enough to live in a sunny part of the world, that will make a big difference. It will also make a big difference if you are at home, consuming power, during daylight hours. Indeed using electricity where it is generated will always be the most efficient solution. In homes, however, energy demands peak around midday and again at 5 pm when we return from school and work. Our

In global environment terms, it doesn't matter who uses solar power, as long as somebody does. For the home owner, without a cost-effective mechanism for selling the solar power you don't need, it will prove to be an expensive gesture.

demand through winter is a third higher than it is in the summer. This, in theory, means that we could meet all our demands in the summer with PV cells, if only our daily demands matched the availability of radiation. Alas this isn't possible in all countries. By 5 pm, the average PV output in the UK drops to a rather low 0.5 kW, falling to nothing shortly after 6 pm. All the energy is harnessed from mid-morning to mid-afternoon, when most are not at home to use it.

Unfortunately, because it isn't practical to store electricity in any usable capacity, at least not without filling a double garage with batteries, our demand for it should ideally coincide with it's delivery to make it really efficient. Of course grid supplied electricity is available 24/7 (bar the occasional power cut), and we are used to it being there whenever it is needed. Renewable-source electricity isn't like that, and if you converted your home solely to solar generated electricity, disconnecting it from the grid, you would have to change your lifestyle dramatically. Between sunset and sunrise, you would have no power at all; in the temperate zones, beneath cloudy winter skies, PV systems may still operate, but generate only small amounts of power, cutting available electricity to a small fraction of its previous level.

Given the present state of the art,

generating more electricity by PV cells would mean covering a greater area with them. More panels equals more power. You can generate about 750 kWh per year per panel in the UK, at least given our traditional climate, but most of that will be available in the summer on bright sunny days. This figure of power production looks a bit lame if you only have one or two panels on your roof, so some roof tile companies have started making tiles that are compatible with PV systems, interlocking with them and blending harmoniously into a unified roof covering that enables you to cover the whole roof to improve the power supply. Some green activists are a little sceptical about the use of PV cells in domestic situations, where the roofs are small and the need for electricity peaks when solar energy isn't available. Because of these two overwhelming drawbacks, they believe that most domestic PV systems only run for about eight per cent of the time, power being drawn from the national grid for the remaining 92 per cent.

Having said all that and laid it on the line for you, most of the well-documented eco-home case builds seem to do very well, even if their occupants live, shall we say, a more 'simplistic' lifestyle than most of us. One home in New Zealand, built in 1998 with a roof dressed by no less than 20 PV panels on a north-facing slope, achieved a capacity of 1.16 kW solar generated output. With a top-up supply from three small wind turbines, which added a mere 100 watts, the owners have reportedly enjoyed living off-grid entirely and have neither had to buy in nor sell electricity. They metered a grand total of 1200 kWh of generated power in a year, which, with some stringent energy-conservation measures, has enabled them to achieve energy liberation. I should point out that the house was wired to use DC current, special appliances being employed to avoid the installation of an inverter, and I have no idea how much battery power they had available after dark. I'm sure it made for a few quiet nights in.

What we could really use at this point in time are some major advances in battery technology that would allow us to store the power, if only for half a day.

Design before install

As with all aspects of home improvement, you need to plan ahead carefully, and in the case of solar systems that planning couldn't be more critical. Luckily the sun follows the same path through the sky on each day of the year, and while the ancients had to drag huge stones into position to reveal the exact point of mid-summer or mid-winter, we have computer programs. In these programs, your home is the stone, across which the sun moves, revealing the hours and level of light falling upon it on each day. Since the roof-top PV cells can't rotate to track the sun's path, for some of the time they will be in shade and less effective, if not totally unemployed. The results of these computations can usually be presented graphically and can be based on hourly changes. Because more cells mean more power, the array on the roof is all important. These arrays have a string order, which is also recognized by the program.

The computer programs use weather databases, can take into account shading from nearby buildings and trees (with or without leaves depending on the season), and are able to make predictions about your electricity consumption, production and costs – usually leading up to that all-important sales moment, the economic payback calculation. This is the information you need to see before committing to an installation.

The problem is that the design is usually only offered by the installer, who will be keen to sell the system to you, and you have to trust them to input all of the correct and relevant data. The information in this design section will at least help you to decide whether you have the basic ingredients in your home for an effective PV system, but the design of it is still crucial.

ORIENTATION

The table (right) shows differences in power outputs of arrays facing in different directions and in different planes. The perfect pitch depends on your latitude, and these examples are based on London, UK. There 30 degrees off the horizontal is optimum; 45 degrees sees a slight reduction in output, while vertical (as in a wall mounted panel) produces a considerable reduction.

Perhaps more than orientation, over-shading is of prime importance. Having a module that is shaded by structures or trees for much of the day will reduce the power output dramatically.

Of course, to get the correct data from the computer program, the correct data has to be entered, and your home has to be surveyed effectively in the process. The critical elements of a survey include the exact orientation of the roof slopes,

HOW MUCH POWER CAN BE CAPTURED FROM THE SUN?

In Egypt, you could expect to generate 1000 watts/sq.m almost daily; in England, 600 would be nearer the mark, given winter sunshine. On average, the solar irradiation for England is 2.6 kWh/sq.m/day, but in the far north of the country, this drops to 2.2.

It doesn't end there. To plot solar irradiation throughout the year, you need to consider the orientation of the PV array's surface and its angle or tilt. Orientation is measured from east (sunrise), through south, to west (sunset) with due south being the maximum exposure. The perfect tilt depends on your latitude, since this determines the path of the sun overhead throughout the year. In London, at 51 degrees, 36 minutes N, a roof pitch of 31 degrees is the perfect angle.

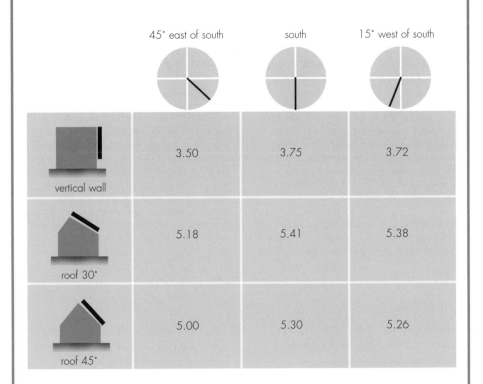

Comparison of array outputs

Ten key points
for a successful installation

1 Remember that although PV arrays will work under cloudy skies, longer sunny periods mean greater power output.

2 Measure your roof pitch and compare it to the optimum pitch for your latitude.

3 Consider the orientation of your roof array. Aim for due south in the northern hemisphere, or as close to it as possible, and due north in the southern hemisphere.

4 Avoid over-shading your PV array. This will reduce its output significantly.

5 Ensure ventilation behind the PV array to remove heat from the modules.

6 Ideally the power generated should be used in the home and not 'exported' to the grid. If you're using a grid-connection system, however, and intend to sell your unwanted power to the electricity company, the annual energy production from the modules is your key figure, not the production that you actually use.

7 Modules do vary in design and appearance, so shop around. Some are integrated with roof tile ranges, and you may want to consider re-covering the roof entirely to blend in the arrays for a seamless installation.

8 Remember that you may be only supplying a small portion of your own electricity demands and selling back the rest, reducing your fuel bills, but also reducing carbon emissions.

9 PV arrays needn't be fitted to your main roof, a single-storey extension or conservatory roof could be converted if it has the necessary exposure to the sun. A PV array makes an ideal solution to cooling an overheated conservatory.

10 Bolt-on installations can compromise the weather resistance of a roof if they aren't fixed properly. Some badly installed arrays have been screwed to the rafters through holes drilled in the roof tiles, relying on silicone mastic to plug the damage and keep out rain. Fixings not only need to be effective at holding the panel down against wind pressure, but also corrosion resistant and weatherproof. A system that offers a whole-roof guarantee of weather resistance is the best choice.

the pitch or angle of the roof, and the distance from and shadowing potential of other buildings and trees.

Given our power demands, a substantial number of panels is essential with a decent sized south-facing (north-facing in the southern hemisphere) roof to house them. In Germany (where they are frequently installed), there are homes with 16 panels on the roof, each capable of generating 80 watts and collectively producing 1000 kWh per year. If you were able to harness all of that production, about a third of your power demands could be met by the sun. Panels are often manufactured in 80 watt sizes, and in a remote location, one of these plus a battery would be sufficient to

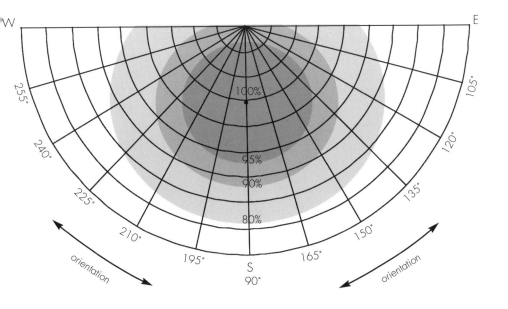

W   E

255°   240°   225°   210°   195°   S   165°   150°   135°   120°   105°
90°

100%

95%

90%

80%

orientation   orientation

Yearly irradiation map for London

power an electric cattle fence or a few lights. For a home in an urban environment, beneath cloudy skies, you would need much more, but nevertheless they are effective, and I am drawn to the thought that if all the new buildings constructed in the last 20 years had incorporated PV systems on their roofs, much of our power need would already have been met by a renewable source of energy.

Modules are rated in Wp, the unit of peak watts, which is the output of power that an array will generate at noon on a sunny day. You need to be aware of that because you can't really base the electricity production forecast on such a rare event. You might, for example, be sold an array that produces 2kWp (2000 kW of peak rated power per year). This means that it will produce significantly less over the whole year, so don't compare the kWp value directly to your power needs and think, 'Whoopee, I can meet two-thirds of my demand!'

INSTALLING PV ARRAYS ON SUN LOUNGE AND CONSERVATORY ROOFS

It is possible to trap PV cells between layers of glass and incorporate a transparent material between the cells to let some light pass through into the room below. The light will have a dappled quality to it, but that could be quite pleasing in the right room, particularly as many south-facing (north-facing in the southern hemisphere) conservatories suffer from overheating, and this would help to shade them. You

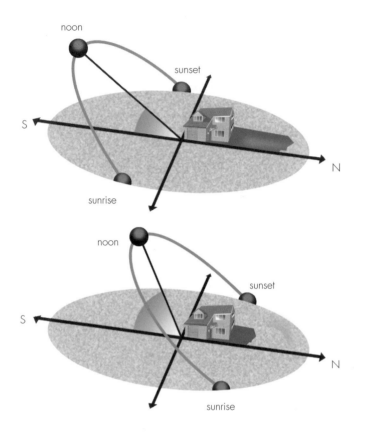

Typical sunpath in winter (above) and summer (below) for temperature latitudes

might be able to solve two problems by converting a sun lounge or conservatory roof to PV arrays, although probably it will be necessary to replace the entire roof structure with one capable of supporting their weight. PV arrays are comparable to glass roofs in weight, but are about five times heavier than polycarbonate sheeting.

If I had to recommend a roof for solar conversion, it would be this type. I know that conservatories are usually low with shallow-pitched roofs, but so many of those I've seen have been uninhabitable in summer because of their exposure to the sun and overheating. If you suffer from this problem and would like to convert your conservatory to a room that you can enjoy all summer, then instead of installing expensive fitted blinds or a power guzzling air conditioner, convert the roof to a solar powered PV array.

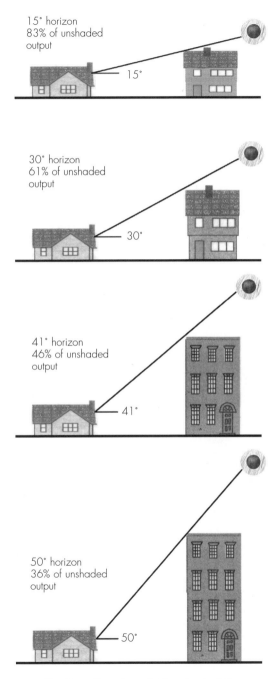

15° horizon
83% of unshaded
output

15°

30° horizon
61% of unshaded
output

30°

41° horizon
46% of unshaded
output

41°

50° horizon
36% of unshaded
output

50°

Shading effects by neighbouring buildings

Increasing the roof pitch to suit will make it drain rainwater much more efficiently, improve the appearance of your home and turn the overheated conservatory into a more habitable room – all as valuable side-effects of generating your own power.

COLOUR CHOICE

Although it would be possible to have coloured cells (other than the standard blue-black), to do so would reduce their efficiency, since the slate colour is ideal for absorbing the sun's rays. Other colours reflect more of the light in varying degrees.

PANEL WEIGHT

The weight of PV solar panels shouldn't be a problem for the structure of most roofs, but if in doubt, add up the total weight and compare it to the weight of the existing tiles. A typical module of crystalline silicon, measuring 0.5 m x 1.2 m and framed, weighs around 7.5 kg, which is about the same as a slate covering of the same area; concrete tiles would be quite a lot heavier.

SIDE EFFECTS

Not surprisingly there will be heat coming off the back of a PV array, generated by convection and radiation working

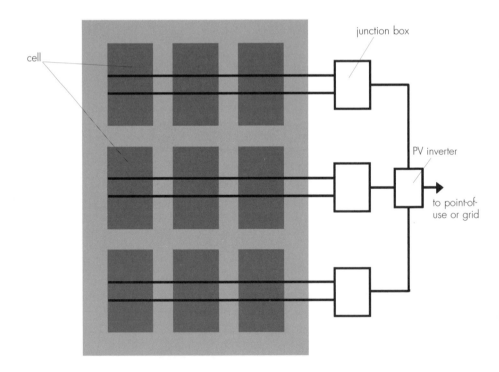

Assembly of a PV module

together. It can be anything between 30 and 45 per cent of the total energy arriving from the sun. Through these same processes, an equal amount flows out through the panel to the surrounding air. A smaller amount of energy may also be reflected back off the surface, typically about eight per cent. Consequently, as a rule, only about 15 per cent is actually employed in electrical output. You can see straight away that there is room for improvement in the efficiency of PV cells. Don't be tempted to compare this figure to today's condensing boilers burning fossil fuels, which run at about 90 per cent efficiency; compare it to the power stations and supply grids that deliver our electricity by burning gas or coal at 35–40% efficiency.

When locating a PV array, you need to bear in mind that some heat will come off the back of it. You certainly don't want to be burning power by running fans in an attempt to cool this space. The panels need some air flow over the back to stop them from overheating, which reduces their efficiency.

They are thought to have a life expectancy of over 20 years, but like any electrical installation, the control units and wiring connections can sometimes need replacing.

METERING

We are all used to one-way metering – the electricity we import from the grid is clocked and we pay for what we use. But with your own mini power station comes a different form of metering – two-way.

Two-way metering can be based on two meters, one for imported electricity and the other for exported electricity produced by your home. This kind of metering is essential where different rates exist for buying and selling electricity, allowing you to deduct the value of the exported power from the price of the imported power.

In some countries, where the price of electricity is the same whether you're buying or selling, you may have a meter that runs backwards when your home is doing the generating, turning back the figures for the power you've previously imported from the grid. The idea of an electricity meter that runs backwards appeals to me, and I could see myself watching that instead of the TV.

PAYBACK TIME

For most of us, the payback time for a PV system is lengthy to say the least, probably 30 years on average. This is largely because electricity is so cheap, even in the UK where, in 2005, it cost about 7p a unit. Compare this to the cost of installing say £20,000 worth of photo-voltaic panels and the fact that these would be likely to generate about 2000 units of electricity in an average British year, saving only £150 on the electricity bill. That means that electricity produced by solar power could cost four or five times more per unit. Wherever you live in the world, it is worth running this calculation, but don't forget that a PV system should also add value to your home, and definitely don't forget that the main reason for installing one is to help protect our environment.

So you can see the problem. You can only reach a 20-year payback if you can take advantage of a 50 per cent government grant and/or the roof needs replacing anyway because it's in a bad state. Ripping off a perfectly good roof to recover it is expensive and not something many of us would want to do. Where payback is increased by cell numbers and climate to many thousands of units per year, the financial benefits make it much more attractive. In southern Spain, for example, where the solar radiation is a third greater than the UK, or in Egypt, where it is more than double, you could halve the payback time easily.

THE FUTURE FOR SOLAR POWER

Because PV arrays work best on a building-by-building basis, the opportunity exists to reduce carbon emissions if we all decided to convert to this system, ending reliance on fossil-fuel-based electricity for good. Because of their sheer number, if all homes supplied electricity to the grid in this way, the problem of sustainable power would be solved. It makes sense, but I feel it won't happen until governments take steps to make such installations more affordable to home owners, thus creating a shorter payback time, or new developments make the products cheaper. It would also help if PV installations were required on all new and renovated commercial buildings through

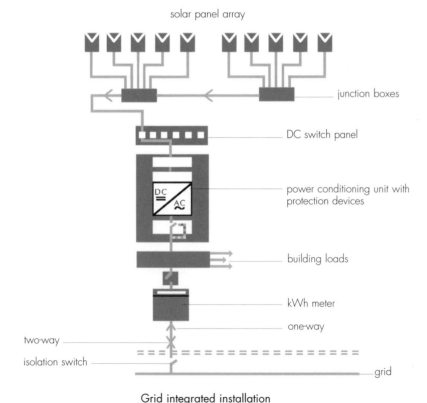

solar panel array

junction boxes

DC switch panel

power conditioning unit with protection devices

building loads

kWh meter

one-way

two-way

isolation switch

grid

Grid integrated installation

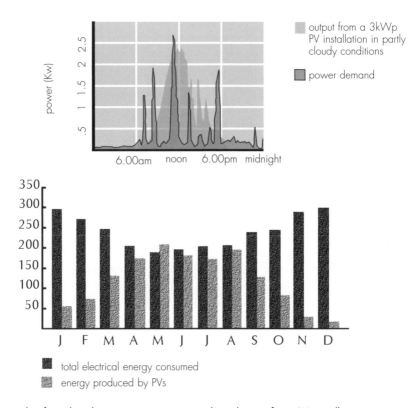

power (Kw)

.5 1 1.5 2 2.5

6.00am   noon   6.00pm   midnight

output from a 3kWp PV installation in partly cloudy conditions

power demand

350
300
250
200
150
100
50

J F M A M J J A S O N D

total electrical energy consumed
energy produced by PVs

Example of predicted power consumption and production for a PV installation

building codes and regulations. With their large roof areas, these buildings have the potential to harness a considerable amount of solar radiation for their own use during daylight hours.

In 2005 Germany and Japan had programmes under way to convert 100,000 and 70,000 homes respectively to solar power. The market for the technology in these countries is more established than in others, such as the UK, where it has been available since 1998, but in a state of virtual obscurity.

Although some governments need to do more to encourage the use of PV cells, especially in countries where exposure to solar radiation is limited by the climate, what we also need are advances in technology to reduce the costs. Hopefully these won't be long in coming. Plastic cells are being developed that could potentially reduce the cost by as much as 95 per cent; with this cost cutting, the floodgates should open on solar power.

Wind power

The wind is regarded as one of the most efficient sources of 'green' energy, and some countries have been using it for some time. Most notable are Denmark and Holland, where wind farms were developed while everybody else was wondering how much longer the gas fields of the North Sea would last. Denmark now produces 20 per cent of its power requirements from the wind. When you approach the eastern coast of Jutland from the North Sea, you can see how this is achieved. Before the coast is visible, you can see the white towers of the turbines lined up, catching the ever-present wind. They have already proved to be a cost-effective way of providing 'green' electricity, and undoubtedly they will become widespread. In some locations, wind is a predictable source as well as a sustainable one.

Coastlines and flatlands are ideal areas for wind turbines, and places like the west coasts of Denmark and the British Isles have seen the construction of wind farms to harvest the wind's energy for grid consumption. Potentially a turbine's tower can reach 200 m high and and its blades 70 m long. Such a giant can generate 5 megawatts of power, but its visual impact on the surrounding landscape is often unacceptable, simply because of its scale. And so wind farms are the subject of government debate; they sit alongside sewerage treatment plants and glue factories as bad neighbours and as developments controlled by environmental law. Yet those 5 megawatt towers are planned for off-shore installation in Germany, where their visual impact will be easier to bear.

If we don't like the idea of these giant towers dominating the landscape, there is an alternative – micro wind turbines on buildings. The tiniest of these are already used on yachts to power the lights, but a step up in size could generate some of your home's power needs without any significant visual impact, beyond that already caused by a TV aerial or a satellite dish.

Home micro wind turbines
EXPOSURE AND ORIENTATION

Although using micro wind turbines to back up domestic electricity supplies may be more acceptable visually than massive wind turbines, would they work? Once again the answer is 'yes' for some and 'no' for others. Like solar power cells, orientation and exposure of the turbine is critical. If you live in a built-up area, not necessarily in a town or city, but simply among other buildings, the chances are it won't work because the wind tends to buffet and spill over rooftops and around walls, creating vortexes and eddies, positive and negative pressure. The same occurs around natural obstructions like woodlands and cliffs. This is the wrong kind of wind for today's wind-turbine technology. Turbines need something called planar wind, which flows straight and level into the propellers, preferably continuously. This means that they need exposure to open space.

The UK for example, although small and crowded, has 9000 miles of coastline and many hills inland that face the coast – a great many homes have the potential for micro wind farming, particularly in the west facing the Atlantic. Cliff tops, though, don't make good sites, as the wind tends to smack into them and ride turbulently to the top and over it. A smooth hill or incline that actually increases the

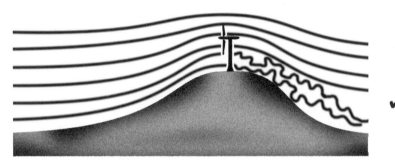

speed up effect over smooth hills is ideal

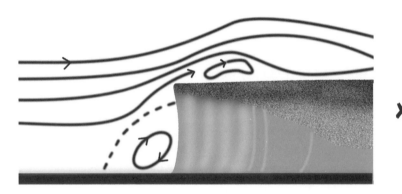

turbulence at top and bottom of cliffs is to be avoided

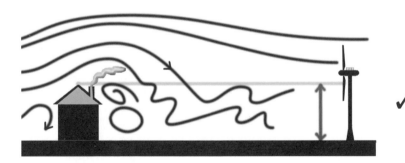

site clear of obstructions by at least 10 x ht of obstruction required

Wind flow and topography – good and bad

speed of the approaching wind in a smooth manner is far better.

MAXIMUM POWER

So if you have the location, how much power can you produce?

In the world of wind turbines, power output is related directly to three design elements: size, weight and noise. All three increase with power, and all three will govern the design and installation of any domestic wind turbine.

The propeller diameter is the principal limitation of any wind turbine. The larger it is, the greater the power capacity of the device. Those wind-farm giants appear to be turning too slowly to generate power, but with 70 m blades, the tip speed is around 100 mph. For domestic use, the blade length must be scaled down to a metre or so, giving a diameter of 2 m – not too large to grace any building. On this scale, the turbine could generate maybe 500 kWh of power every year, around ten per cent of the home's needs. It may prove more acceptable visually to install two slightly smaller turbines on opposite ends of a roof, which together could gather a quarter of your power needs.

If these figures seem disappointing, remember that in an integrated system, you will be selling power back to the energy company, reducing your electricity bill as well as providing some free power for yourself. Bear in mind, too, that the wind is as unpredictable as the sun, and neither appears on demand.

The turbine's power rating is based on tests at a fixed wind speed, perhaps around 10 m/sec.

A single home wind turbine might only generate 1kW of power; two of them would generate the same power as about 30 standard PV solar panels.

As with solar power, you have the choice of an off-grid installation or an integrated set-up that will draw power from the grid when the wind isn't blowing and the batteries have been exhausted. Excess power can also be exported back to the grid, but only if the installation has been approved by the supplying electricity company. It is likely that, as well as setting the technical standards for the installation, the company will limit the turbine size and the amount of power generated. Electrical protection equipment is vigorously regulated to ensure safety in all electrical installations, and in this field it is even more important. Wind turbines suitable for domestic use are quite cheap in themselves (at least when compared to photo-voltaic arrays), but the costs of installation and connection to the main supply grid can be very high.

WEIGHT AND APPEARANCE

Made from fibreglass and aerodynamically optimized in shape, the smallest domestic wind turbines are quite light in weight. At around 30 kg, most are nearly half the weight of a square metre of clay or concrete roof tiles, and normally this isn't a problem for supporting from a gable end wall of your home. Careful mounting of the mast with several expansion bolts, or better still resin anchor fixings, set in the masonry will ensure that it doesn't vibrate loose in operation. A sound chimney stack could also be employed to support a short mast provided its masonry is in sound condition. The height of the

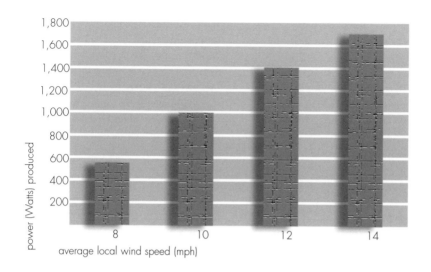

Monthly energy estimates based on wind speeds

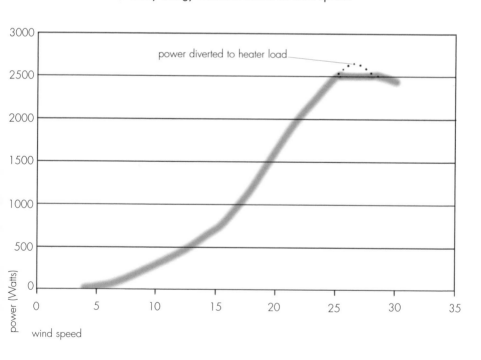

Estimated power production based on wind speed (showing cut off at max. speed)

stack is important though. A chimney that is four times or more its width in height will be too slender. If it projects 2 m above the masonry, then it should also extend to half that distance alongside the chimney to ensure a solid fixing distributed down the masonry. Remember that the turbine is a dynamic machine, so if you are at all in doubt about the quality of the masonry or strength of fixing, seek the advice of a structural engineer.

We are all becoming used to seeing the vertical-axis types in giant wind-farm form, but micro turbines come in both vertical- and horizontal-axis types. The latter look a lot like weather vanes and the former, of course, resemble an aircraft's propeller.

In many countries, planning permission is needed for the installation of a wind turbine, even of a small domestic size, but increasingly government support is creating policies that favour them. Even to the point of allowing them in national parks, areas of outstanding natural beauty and other places where, for example, a satellite dish would be wholly unacceptable, as long as they are small-scale and not seriously detrimental to the environment.

In most areas, micro turbines are likely be restricted to an output of 1.5kW to be acceptable, not only structurally, but also aesthetically and audibly. At this size, the blades are very thin and may be only 600 or 700 mm in length, the weight will be about 28 kg and the decibel production around 70 decibels.

The downside, of course, is that this power output is the maximum potential and not the average. For much of the time, the turbine may produce nothing

at all. Although it would have the potential to equal 18 PV solar panels, the wind is not as predictable as daylight. So micro turbines can only contribute towards our electricity needs, rather than supplying them completely. They would need installing on a grand scale to have any real chance of slowing global warming.

NOISE

One of the primary objections to wind farms is the noise they create. Large turbines make an incessant noise in operation, and the small ones don't run silently either. If anything, noise becomes more critical in the case of small-scale domestic turbines. In normal operation, however, some models produce a fairly high running noise of around 80 decibels – about the same amount of noise generated by road traffic. Noise, of course, reduces as your distance from the source increases, and since most domestic turbines are likely to be fixed at least 8 m from ground level, the effect of the noise will be reduced. Location, while primarily determined by exposure to the wind, should also reflect this. An 80 decibel turbine whining away outside your bedroom window will keep you awake at

Wind turbine kits are now available complete with 'plug and play' technology, reducing installations costs dramatically. Connected to your home's power circuit via a standard plug, like any other appliance, they make it quicker and easier to install.

blades
powerhead
nacelle
spinner
tail fin
tail boom

Wind turbine

night if you haven't got good sound insulation. As far as I can tell, even the most beautifully sculpted fibreglass models with 1 m blades that generate less than 1 kW, produce sound levels of up to 35 decibels in full speed. You can reduce the problem by selecting a model with a stalling mechanism to protect against over-speeding. This doesn't seem to raise the noise level in the same way that a 'flutter' mechanism does.

Noise pollution is another reason why wind turbines are better suited to remote detached homes with some land around them than small urban properties. Not only will the wind turbulence around built-up areas create the wrong aerodynamics, but the noise produced will be unwanted by your neighbours.

Although a rotor diameter of around 2 m might sound too big for your roof, remember that the blades are usually very slender, as is the main body. Placing one on a mast erected from the gable end apex would site the turbine axis 2 m above the ridge line of the roof, which is likely to be at least another 2 m above the windows. Some space separation would be achieved, which would reduce the noise intrusion. Aesthetically, seeing wind turbines on our

Ten expert tips
for converting to wind power

1 Location, location, location – get to know your neighbourhood, determine the direction of the prevailing wind and decide if your roof is sheltered from it by other buildings, trees or the landscape itself. It is a good idea to record the wind speed and direction for some time beforehand.

2 House or tower? – if you can't use a gable end at roof level to support a turbine mast and you have enough land, consider erecting a tower away from your home, bearing in mind that it will need a substantial amount of space. Not only because of its visual impact, but also for maintenance. It is one thing to put a ladder against the wall of your home, but quite another to put it against a thin tubular tower, so most domestic turbine towers need to be lowered for maintenance; they simply aren't robust enough to be climbed.

3 Siting – exposure to the wind is important. The turbine should be aligned with a planar wind that arrives in a smooth flow. Sites facing level ground, a smooth hill or open water are ideal. At all costs, avoid placing it where it will be buffeted by turbulent wind.

4 Design and installation specialists – it is worth employing a specialist company that will carry out both tasks after a site survey. The benefits should come in large and small details, like selecting the correct specification and size of cable. Electricians inexperienced in wind-turbine installations may not be used to working with such low-voltage supplies.

5 Planning permission – check whether you require planning permission for the installation. You'll need to submit details of the turbine itself, its size and its proposed position to the planning authority.

6 Maintenance – remember that in addition to the installation costs, you will have to bear the cost of maintaining the turbine and repairing it from time to time. Look for a five-year guarantee from the manufacturer to reduce maintenance costs.

7 Integrated systems – even on the most perfect windy site, a turbine with a rotor diameter of 5 m or more would be necessary to meet all your electricity needs, so don't be too optimistic about how much you can produce. Aim to generate a percentage of your power with an integrated system and compare it with solar power.

8 Running speed – to get full-power efficiency from your turbine, the shaft speed must be more than 2000 rpm (revolutions per minute). On a large wind-

homes will take some time to get used to, but we have accepted TV satellite dishes, so I'm sure they will become a normal part of the townscape one day.

COMPONENTS

The typical component parts of a turbine are shown in an illustration (see page 51).

Essentially you have a spinning nose cone behind which the blades are located. The alternator and nacelle (for converting AC to DC current if required) make up the power head that collects the energy and balances the turbine aerodynamically, at least for the vertical-axis types. A tail boom and fin extend farm turbine, the shaft is geared to produce this speed from blades that turn much slower; on a micro turbine, the short blades will spin much faster.

9 Efficiency – high-efficiency generators are at the core of wind turbines. Often the wind speed isn't very high, and the gearing mechanism needed to compensate for this reduces efficiency. A good generator is essential. In a light breeze, almost all the energy can be expended in producing a magnetic field in the alternator. Wind-farm generators use permanently magnetized motors to overcome this.

10 Noise level – check the manufacturer's sound tests for the turbine to see how much noise it produces, not only in normal operation, but also in over-speed protection. Most turbines have an over-speed protection system. Some use sideways furling or yaw to create instability, or 'flutter', in the turbine if it starts to run too fast in a gale. In essence the turbine becomes unaerodynamic to protect itself from running too fast. When this happens, the turbine noise level can increase dramatically. Noise levels are worth looking in to carefully. Consider the distance from other buildings and the sound insulation in your home's walls and windows.

behind the power head, creating the appearance of a model aircraft.

ELECTRICAL INSTALLATION PROBLEMS

One of the principal requirements with a wind turbine is to limit the speed and with it the power generated. Some models have a built-in circuit breaker (CB) for the turbine's input, while others rely on a fused connection-unit switch on the incoming supply. Protective devices like these are essential and will be specified by local electrical safety regulations. The manufacturer will guide you on cable sizing for the turbine, which will be affected by a maximum length of run. A maximum current is always stipulated for each model, measured in amps. A typical 1 kW turbine may have a maximum current rating of 60 amps for example. A polarity test is important on the wiring to ensure that the positive and negative wires are correctly connected; the electrician carrying out the installation should carry out this test.

TOWER INSTALLATIONS

A turbine needn't be attached to a building; it can be mounted on a freestanding tower. Away from the home, a tower can be erected in the garden where it may create less visual impact and noise pollution. Height is the issue here – the higher the tower, the greater the chance of the turbine receiving clean flowing wind. The height of the tower will vary according to the landscape and exposure, but it could be anything from 8 m to 30 m. At the top of the scale, it would be four times the height of a typical two-storey house, and you would need a considerable amount of open space to accommodate it. Most need supporting guy wires that splay out to the surrounding ground for stability, and a 30 m mast could have wires fixed at a 20 m radius at ground level. In effect this would create a 40 m circular footprint. The shortest towers would be closer to the height of a two-storey home, and the radius would be nearer 5 m, creating a footprint of 10 m diameter.

Although the entire site doesn't require a base for the installation's stability, the tower itself requires a foundation, while the guy wires will need anchoring to something substantial. Normally the tower should sit on a small, reinforced-concrete base that will be resistant to ground movement. Any seasonal movement of the subsoil, such as clay heave or shrinkage, will cause the guy wires to slacken and may cause the tower to lean.

All but the shortest towers will need winching into position, having been assembled flat on the ground, so space must be available to do this. You should be getting the picture now that they are not designed for small urban gardens.

Towers that are less than 10 m high can be erected without winching if they have a gin-pole attached to the base to act as a lever. Even with this feature, it takes three or four people and a great deal of care to get the thing upright safely. A pulling force of some 400 kg would be required on the raising cable, even with a gin-pole lever to help. With the tallest towers, that force can exceed 1.5 tonnes, hence the need for a winch.

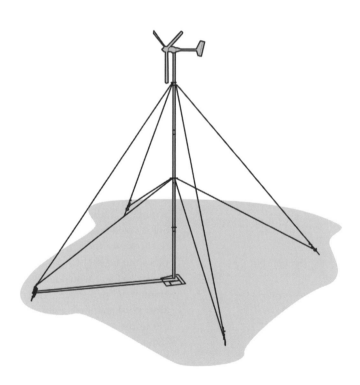

Mast structure with guide wire stabilisers

Regardless of the turbine perched on top, such towers are subject to planning controls. They also demand space separation from other structures and overhead power lines, equal to at least one-and-a-half times their height, to prevent them from causing damage if they collapse. Thus a 10 m tower should be located at least 15 m from your home. Towers are not normally affected by building regulations and codes, however, and are treated as exempted structures in most countries when space separated.

Towers are typically lightweight, scaffold-like affairs resembling miniature electricity pylons – they aren't always pretty. Farms with land and wide open spaces will continue to employ towers for their turbines, since they allow the use of larger-output models, but for the home-improvement market they often aren't viable.

Biomass power

What is biomass? To put it simply, rotting vegetation and animal matter. Trees, plants, creatures, us included, decompose and release carbon at the end of life – carbon that continues in the cycle to appear somewhere else later. Apparently carbon molecules live more or less forever, so in a biologically microscopic way we are all going to be reincarnated. There is some potential in the decomposition process, however, for energy to be harnessed. Methane gas is produced by landfill sites and sewage treatment plants, while ethanol is generated by the fermentation process, and these by-products of anaerobic digestion are sources of fuel. That fuel could have many uses, one of which is to power steam driven

> If biomass fuel is available locally, consider installing an additional storage tank similar to that used for heating oil. The fuel may soon be usable by some standard oil boilers as a 'green' alternative anyway. Used to power a suitable generator, it could be employed to produce electricity for your home, reducing your on-grid consumption. See Chapter 3 for information on oil storage.

generators that produce electricity.

When I first looked at biomass renewables, they all seemed highly unlikely, but I couldn't have been more wrong. It turns out that in the USA, the use of biomass fuels has been growing quietly to the point where the most fuel productive crops are being farmed to supply the raw materials. Switchgrass, sugar cane and corn are good for biomass fuel and are being harvested purely so that they can be fermented to produce ethanol. This is used in vehicle fuel. Used alone in converted engines, not only is it a green renewable fuel, but also it burns cleaner than oil, creating less air pollution. It can also be added to existing petroleum to clean it up a bit without having to convert existing cars to run on it.

You may have read newspaper reports of people avoiding fuel tax altogether by using sunflower oil or some other biological equivalent made from vegetable oils, fat and grease to run diesel engines. It turns out that some of these will run on 'biodiesel' without any conversion, whereas petrol (gasoline) engines will only consume a mixture of about ten per cent ethanol and 90 per cent standard petrol. This blended mix does reduce pollution, but the biodiesel cuts down on virtually everything – carbon dioxide, carbon monoxide, unburnt hydrocarbons and sulphur oxide. There may be a slight increase in nitrogen oxide released in vehicle exhaust emissions, otherwise pollutants are reduced and it would clean up the air in our cities enormously; indeed this has already happened in some where bio-diesel buses are in operation.

So if biomass fuel does become widely available, we should be able to use it not only in our vehicles, but also in our homes. If your home runs on heating oil, converting it to bio-oil shouldn't be difficult. Storage tanks and boilers may not need much conversion to run on such fuels, and I hope it won't belong before boiler manufacturers start producing bio boilers that can burn these products.

Other fuels can also be harvested from biomass. Methane gas is given off by green waste as it decomposes, and landfill sites that have taken most of our vegetable and garden waste suffer from released methane. The gas is a threat to our homes if we allow it to escape through the ground: it can collect beneath floors and in basements, where only a tiny amount is required in the air for it to reach an explosive state. It is expensive to seal buildings close to landfill sites to prevent this from happening, and by 'close', I mean up to 250 m, possibly twice that distance. Methane migrates through the ground using fissures in chalk and other fractured subsoils to aid its journey. On landfill sites and natural marshland where it occurs, it has been common practice to vent it into the atmosphere where it combines with other greenhouse gases. If we could collect it and pipe it away for production, this gas could be used to produce electricity. Sewage treatment plants generate a plentiful supply of methane gas, which they can harvest to meet their own electricity needs. Similarly farms have a generous supply of manure and waste vegetation that can be collected for use in waste-to-energy plants.

I'm not suggesting that biomass technology is suitable for producing electricity on a domestic scale; it isn't. Indeed the major problem with the idea is that you need a large mass to create a small amount of fuel. Where biomass runs into trouble is in the land space it requires – if all nations switched to growing crops for fuel as well as for food, we could kiss goodbye to the rainforests and wilderness areas of the world, which are already threatened by agriculture. The power plants needed for biomass electricity seem to have a minimum economic production of around 400 kW, but are mostly built on the megawatt scale. They are for communities rather than individual homes, although farm estates could certainly use them to operate off-grid.

For most of us, there isn't a 'green' solution that will allow us to live totally off-grid without compromising our lifestyle, but in most homes there is a way of reducing the demand for on-grid electricity and cutting the electricity bill significantly.

Small changes, big differences

Installing an alternative power source isn't an option for everyone, but that doesn't mean you can't reduce your power demand. Minor alterations and the use of technology can help, such as employing PIR switching to ensure that lights are never left on unnecessarily and selecting the most efficient appliances when you are replacing them. Making some changes to your lifestyle can take you even farther.

● OPT FOR SOLAR POWERED
   GARDEN LIGHTS

Installing solar powered garden lights is a much better option than choosing a conventional low-voltage garden lighting kit. Although 12 volt garden lighting may be safe, it is not energy-efficient. If existing low-voltage lights haven't already given up on you because a mouse has chewed through the thin cable or the tiny bulbs have become damp, replace them with some quality solar powered lamps. Site them to illuminate path edges and features so that you can appreciate them every evening in the early hours of darkness before you turn in. Solar lights are a big improvement, although they don't create a huge amount of light because they tend to employ small LEDs as the light source for efficiency and clean white light.

● AVOID STAND-BY DEVICES

Those little red lights that indicate something, usually the TV, is simply resting and waiting for us to press a button for it to spring into action do mean that the power is still on and being consumed – in a much greater quantity than you might imagine. Turn off all such appliances at the switch.

● REDUCE CONSUMPTION

Converting your home to eco-friendliness is about taking measures that allow you to carry on living while your home takes care of you, not the other way around. Part of that means switching to energy-efficient white goods. Kitchen appliances have to be energy rated, so seek out the best ratings. In the USA, they use 'energy star' ratings; in EC Europe the A to G banding system.

ENSURING APPLIANCE EFFICIENCY

● In fridge/freezers, heavy doors with a good seal are essential.

● In dishwashers, less water consumption means less cost to operate. Look for the least amount of water per wash cycle. It is possible to find the top-end of energy ratings with

---

UNDERSTANDING THE UNITS OF ENERGY

It is very easy to become confused by the units of energy measurement, but this table explains them.

Joule (J) – The unit of energy. 1 joule is the amount of energy needed to heat 1 gramme of air by 1 degree or raise 1 kg by 10 cm.

Watt (W) – The unit of power. A measurement of the rate at which energy is transferred: 1 watt is equal to the consumption of 1 joule of energy per second. So a 60 watt light bulb burns at the rate of 60 joules per second. A kilowatt (kW) is 1000 watts.

Kilowatt hour (power x time) – A measurement of quantity and not a rate. 1 kWh is the total energy used if we consume it at the rate of 1 kW in one hour. It is a rate (kW) multiplied by a time (h) that gives us a quantity. So a 60 watt light bulb burning for one hour consumes 0.06 kWh. Joules could be used instead of Kwh, but this unit has become the standard.

Plug-in energy meter

these. If you can use a lower temperature setting do so, but not if it means washing dishes twice.

● In washing machines, front loading, water-level controls (to reduce water consumption), adjustable spin cycles and large capacities for plenty of clothes per wash are all desirable features ensuring energy efficiency. Half-load washes are a waste of power.

● In tumble-dryers, look for a large capacity and always load to the full. Half-loads waste power.

● Using appliances with built-in timers and programmers will help you to take advantage of cheaper off-peak electricity, helping to reduce your electricity bill.

● A plug-in energy meter can be programmed to compute the actual cost of any appliance over a given period. Those with clear LCD digital read-outs are best. You can move them from appliance to appliance to discover the heaviest power consumers, enabling you to control their use. These 'smart' meters are a perfect way to begin conserving your power.

CHAPTER THREE

Heat

Heating buildings requires a lot of energy. As an example, 40 per cent of the UK's energy is consumed in heating its buildings, and that is responsible for a hefty proportion of the carbon emissions we are having such a problem in reducing. Because of this, insulation requirements have increased steadily to try to put the brakes on this carbon pollution, but there is a limit to how much lagging we can stuff in our lofts. Ideally we need to look at other sources for our heating and hot water, in combination with better insulation.

It will not have escaped your notice that the sun is the principle source of heat on the planet. It has been burning for the last 4.6 billion years, shows no sign of stopping and is the reason why we – and all life – are here at all. Given that, it is very difficult to understand why we haven't been capturing its energy, and employing it to heat our homes and provide us with the hot water we all need.

Perhaps now is the time to start.

Solar energy for hot water

The use of solar technology for heating water isn't new; it just hasn't been popular in the past. And it hasn't been popular for three reasons: one, too few of us had a reason for using it; two, the industry suffered from some retro-fit cowboys who damaged its reputation; and three, the collection panels were of the evacuated-tube type that looked rather like huge propagators bolted to the roof.

Now we have a reason to install them –

If your home is in a sunny climate and you don't have much need for space heating, solar energy can be just as effective for heating a swimming pool.

the technology has improved and the panels look a lot smarter, and apart from being eco-friendly, they will save money. At long last, using solar energy for heating water makes sense. It is an excellent way of reducing your effect on the environment and a very good way of reducing your fuel bills. By far the most common method of hot water production is to fire up the boiler and store the hot water in a cylinder for use later. Unfortunately heating water by traditional boilers burning gas, oil or electricity is costly and harmful to the environment as well. Using the sun to heat water for free makes a lot of sense.

SUNNY SKIES

In countries like Australia and Spain, rooftop solar water cylinders have been commonplace for many years. In such regions, where the sun's energy is in abundance, the technology employed can be quite basic. Integral collector and storage systems are very simple but effective. Those silver tanks you see on the roofs, which resemble aluminium cylinders, are water tanks. Basically the sun hits the collector, which supplies the storage tank attached directly to it with the heated water. Designed as integral collector/storage systems, these units are also referred to as 'batch water heater units'. They are, of course, only suitable for use in areas where there is no risk of the water freezing due to low temperatures. Such integral systems are cheap and effective, particularly now when some of those countries are making solar energy production mandatory.

In 2005 it became law in Spain for any new or renovated building to be fitted with a solar panel. In introducing this regulation, the Spanish government has advised householders that they can cut their water heating bills by up to 70 per cent just by using one 2 sq.m solar panel. That is a conservative estimate, however; in parts of Spain, it is likely to be much higher.

CLOUDY SKIES

For those of us living under more cloudy skies, the statistics aren't too disappointing either, but a bit more technology has to be employed. In Northern Europe you might expect a lot of seasonal variation in the generation of solar heated water. In the summer, at least 80-90 per cent of all your hot water needs could be met, but in the spring and autumn that could drop to 40-50 per cent, and in the winter, when your hot water demands are a little higher, that could fall again to 10-15 per cent. I know of people who have converted to solar hot water and claim that from May to September their boilers lay dormant, saving them money not only on fuel, but also on eventual maintenance costs.

If you reject an integral system because of the risk of freezing or purely for aesthetic reasons, you have the choice of a pumped system – where the water is circulated through the collector by an electric pump – or a self-pumping system. The latter works by phase changing liquid to vapour, forcing the liquid in the collector to circulate and moving the heat with it to the storage tank. These systems are sometimes called passive, as they don't rely on pumps.

Is your home suitable for conversion to solar hot water?

YES if you have:

● A roof slope of at least 4 sq.m in area facing between south-east and south-west (northern hemisphere; north-east and north-west in southern

storage container

solar panel

Batch water heater unit

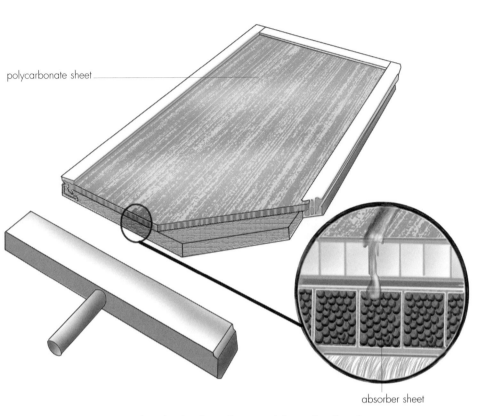

polycarbonate sheet

absorber sheet

Low cost drain-back solar collector with heat absorber sheet

hemisphere) and pitched between 21 and 45 degrees. A solar collecting panel of about 2.75 sq.m could meet at least 50 per cent of the annual hot water demand for two people over the course of a year. In sunnier climates, that could rise to 90 per cent or more. With a larger panel (4 sq.m), three or four people could achieve the same.

● Space for the hot water storage cylinder – if not in a room, then in the attic.

● A mains voltage supply (fused socket outlets) near the cylinder to power the solar pump and control. (Some models also come complete with immersion heaters for emergency back-up heating.)

● Sufficient mains water pressure (at least 1.5 bar, but subject to manufacturers' requirements). Your water supply company can advise you of the pressure.

● At least 300 mm between the bottom of the collector panel and the cylinder.

61

● A conventional (not combi) boiler or electric heater as a back-up when solar energy is low.

Solar collector panels

A good place to start is at the top by choosing the right solar panel for your home. One that supplies your energy needs, fits your budget and looks like it belongs on your roof.

Most collectors are between 1.8 and 5.5 sq.m in area, and with the amount of energy produced (depending on their size) ranging from 18 to 60 MJ per day, you can assume that area and energy output run hand in hand. The vast majority of domestic panels are 2 or 3 m in area. A 2 sq.m collector, say 1 m wide and 2 m high, would have a potential output of about 20 MJ/ day or, to put

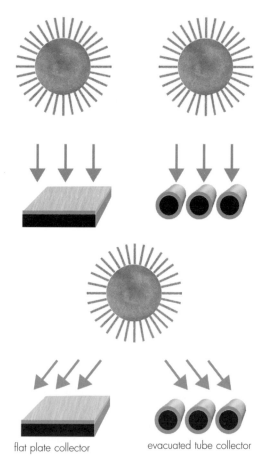

flat plate collector   evacuated tube collector

Solar collectors vary in performance with orientation. Flat plate collectors operate best when the sun is directly overhead, the evacuated tube collector can work optimally throughout the day as the tubes are always perpendicular to the sun's rays.

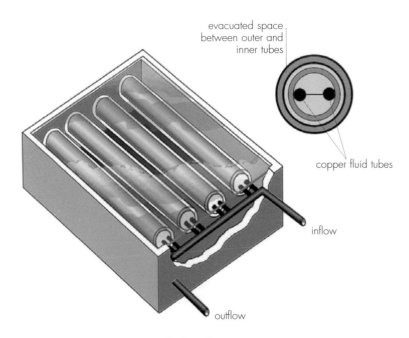

evacuated space
between outer and
inner tubes

copper fluid tubes

inflow

outflow

Evacuated-tube collector

simply, it could heat 450 litres of water every day. This is a standard installation, and you would need to find a sunny spot on your roof of at least that area.

Orientation makes all the difference to exposure, as does the slope of the roof. Due south in the northern hemisphere (due north in the southern), with a roof slope angle that places it perpendicular to the path of the sun in spring and autumn is ideal. The sun's path varies with latitude and the seasons if you don't live on the equator. Some panels are adjustable in tilt and can be raised in winter to cope with the sun's lower path through the sky. Such elevated panels are at risk from wind uplift, however, which makes them more suited, if not restricted, to sheltered locations. Although they are popular on low-rise North American homes, this is not

the case in Europe.

In the past, collection panels weren't very attractive, but today some of them look no different to a glass rooflight or the roof of a conservatory, presenting a slimmer profile than before. These are known as flat-plate collectors. Their predecessors, the evacuated-tube type, are still available, and it is worth comparing the two.

EVACUATED-TUBE COLLECTORS

This technology has been with us for many years and is tried and tested for heating water. Although some fine tuning has occurred in recent years to integrate it with modern plumbing systems, it remains basically the same. It is most effective in this role, even beneath cloudy skies. The owners of the last two homes I inspected that had been converted to solar hot

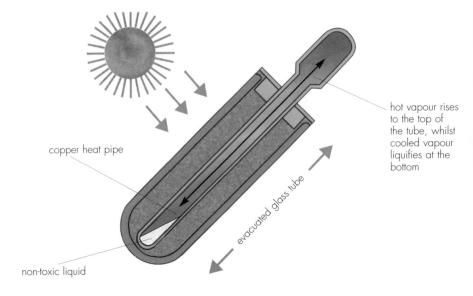

hot vapour rises to the top of the tube, whilst cooled vapour liquifies at the bottom

copper heat pipe

evacuated glass tube

non-toxic liquid

Evacuated-tube structure

water had encountered problems finding converted plumbers. Even those they employed to install the panels were not convinced that enough heat would be generated to match a boiler and found it hard to see how simply allowing cold water to flow through a glass panel on the roof would raise the water temperature enough, until that is they burned their hands on the collector return pipes. Then they realized that the water was actually too hot and that thermostatic taps would have to be fitted to limit the water temperature flowing from them and protect users from scalding burns. The sun has more than enough energy to heat water.

Evacuated-tube collectors tend to produce hotter water than other collectors because of the way they work. Comprising of a series of glass inner and outer tubes arranged in a row, each

containing a heat pipe at their core, the collectors absorb the sun's energy and transfer it to a liquid medium. The air separating the inner and outer tubes is evacuated to prevent heat loss through it, allowing almost all of the sun's energy to be absorbed by the copper heat pipe inside. The non-toxic liquid in the heat pipe does the rest when the hot vapour rises by conduction to the top, while cooled vapour liquefies and sinks to the bottom to become heated again – and so a cycle is created.

Apart from the vacuum void, another advantage of the tubes over the flat-plate type lies in their geometry. Tubes have a surface area that always faces the sun as it arcs across the sky because some part of their surface is always perpendicular to it. Flat panels lose some efficiency by only being perpendicular to the sun at a particular time; the rest of the time, some energy is deflected from them. Because of these features, manufacturers of evacuated-tube collectors claim possible efficiency improvements of up to 40 per cent over the flat-plate type, but that's marketing for you – the new flat-plates are almost as efficient.

FLAT-PLATE COLLECTORS

Despite all that is great about evacuated tubes, I prefer the flat-plate collectors. They perform slightly less efficiently than the former, but they are much cheaper, look a hell of a lot better, are more robust and are easier to install. They come in either a glazed or unglazed form. Either way they have the same basic ingredients: two plate sheets between which water flows to be heated by the sun. In the better-quality models, those sheets may be made of stainless steel, making them longer lasting. The water that flows between them is often mixed with anti-freeze and serves to transfer heat to a storage cylinder rather than being usable hot water.

It has been discovered that if the water flows turbulently rather than smoothly across a flat surface, it can absorb the heat much more effectively. Accordingly some flat-plates have a textured pattern of squares or dimples stamped on to the surface, which always has a matt black finish. This ensures that as little energy as possible is reflected back. The pattern on one plate offsets the pattern on the other, so that they overlap rather than align to send the water cascading between them.

The object is to absorb the heat, trap it between the plates and let the water flowing between them be heated by it. A typical panel would have a collecting area of 2 sq.m. You could expect a glazed panel of this size to weigh about 60 kg, which is mainly due to the glass. That is roughly the same weight as 1 sq.m of concrete roof tiles.

Glazed versions are covered by a single sheet of solar glass, usually with a low iron content, and coated to reduce reflection and glare. In this form the panels take on the appearance of skylight windows, framed in metal, although you can't see through them. If you were thinking how good it would be if we could achieve both transparency and solar absorption, and build a conservatory that provides hot water as well, I'm afraid there is a conflict of principles here. Hot water needs to be supplied at a high temperature to serve our domestic needs, and to get that temperature from the sun we need light-impenetrable black material to absorb its energy. Clear glass panels of double glazing are good for letting the sunlight through, but much of the heat comes through in the form of radiation along with it. The glass absorbs only a small percentage of the sun's energy, which is why many conservatories overheat in the sun. It isn't possible to achieve both.

Hot water is typically heated in a boiler to around 60°C before being pumped around the heating system or sent to our taps. For effective space heating by water filled steel radiators, that is a necessary temperature, but for space heating through an underfloor heating system, the temperature can be less, and for hot water to wash in, it can be much less. Indeed we often have to fit thermostatic taps and showers in our homes to reduce the water temperature to around 43°C so that we can wash safely without burning our skin. Flat plate collectors will work less effectively than evacuated tubes under cloudy skies, heating water to lower temperatures; but since our tap water is preferred at 43°C this is not necessarily a bad thing.

Two south-facing panels are sufficient to serve even a large home, but if all you have is an east- or west-facing roof slope, you might have to add one or two more to get the same result. Choose a selective surface panel with a special coating to minimize re-emission of solar energy. With this coating, these are only a little less efficient than the evacuated-tube type.

COMPARING ENERGY OUTPUTS

Aside from their aesthetic qualities, collectors should also be chosen for their efficiency. This can be defined as how much it will cost to provide the energy output you need. Given the same

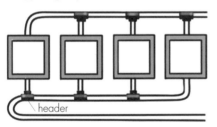

reverse return system

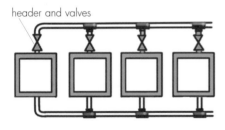

balancing valves system

Collector arrays

energy output for each design, it should be possible to compare the cost of installation if not maintenance. Joules of energy are usually measured per collector per day in this simple calculation, where output is divided by cost of installation. The highest result wins as the expression of how much energy will be available to you per unit of currency.

The only drawback is that the manufacturers of solar collectors will have assessed their energy output under test conditions, almost certainly perfect test conditions, so you can't assume these figures will be achieved in your home. Use them only to compare one against another.

COLLECTOR ARRAYS

If one solar collector is not enough for your home, perhaps because you want to run some space heating from your store of hot water, it is possible to have an array of collectors on the roof. Typically they would be connected by manifolds into a parallel-flow configuration. If balancing valves aren't used to adjust the flow manually, maintaining the flow rate through each collector can be a problem with three or more collectors. The alternative to fitting balancing valves is to plumb them into a reverse return system.

Solar collectors are so productive, however, that one or, at most two, correctly positioned will be more than sufficient for a typical home.

COLLECTOR INSTALLATION PROBLEMS

Since solar panels are invariably roof mounted and involve some penetration of the roof covering, if badly installed, they have the potential to cause the roof to leak and also to cause structural damage. In the past collectors have been surface fitted rather badly on to the roofs of homes, bolted proud over the tiling, often in large panels and they have frightened a lot of people away from alternative energy. It doesn't have to be like that.

AVOIDING COMMON INSTALLATION FAULTS

● Check that the collector has been designed for the wind loads in your location. These vary considerably from the periodic hurricanes around the Gulf of Mexico to the gentler winds experienced by the sheltered inner cities of central Europe; the manufacturer's design loads may not be enough in your location. Local

Ground panels with adjustable angle support can be vulnerable to wind damage

authority building control departments and building codes can be consulted to check on local wind load requirements.

● Look for stainless steel or aluminium metal elements that are corrosion resistant. Galvanized steel isn't always enough in aggressive environments of high humidity, rainfall or salt-laden air. This is particularly important where mounting bolts and nuts are concerned; stainless steel is essential.

● Bolt-on solar collectors should be mechanically fixed to the roof rafters or decking, with sealant membranes and pads used on the fixings.

● Insecure bolting because of insufficient tightening or missing nuts will always lead to problems.

● Make sure that the drain-down pipes have sufficient fall on them to allow the collectors to be drained efficiently to prevent freezing and allow maintenance to be carried out.

● Some collectors replace a section of roof covering and have effective lead flashing kits to seal them to the

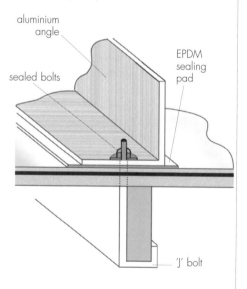

Bracket mounted fixings can leak if sealings aren't employed

covering at the perimeter. In this respect they can be likened to rooflights; the flashing kits should be compared with these when judging their ability to resist wind driven rain. Flashing types depend on the profile of the roof covering.

● Over-roof models that sit above the roof leave the pipes to penetrate the covering. These require flashings that are designed to sleeve the pipes and seal them to the roof. Any 'on site' sealing with silicone mastic and the like is prone to leak soon after, given the extreme temperature variations experienced on roofs.

PAYBACK TIME

Without question solar hot water is the most cost effective of all the renewable technologies for homes. It has the shortest payback time of them all, because during the summer, it can meet all of your hot water needs, as long as it is correctly located and sized. Of course in temperate climates, the winter can see a big reduction in hot water generation, perhaps down to 15–20 per cent of your needs, and that is why you must have a back-up system you can rely on. Even allowing for a dull winter, a solar installation should provide two-thirds of your annual hot water demand, which means it could pay for itself in anything from five to ten years. Of course it depends on the price of fuel during the payback time and, as we know, with oil in particular the price can be volatile. Installers should be able to give you conservative payback calculations if you provide them with information on your

hot water demand and fuel bills. During the summer months, if your heating is switched off and the boiler only fires for hot water, it is a good time to look at your fuel bill; your needs shouldn't change that much throughout the year, but you might add 20 per cent to allow for an unexpected tendency to bathe more often.

If you can achieve 100 per cent of your hot water by solar power in the summer, you should achieve a payback time inside eight years, shorter than that obtained by replacing your windows with double-glazed units. The latter is usually based on ten years.

Types of system
INDIRECT HOT WATER SYSTEMS

An indirect hot water system is one in which hot water is stored in a cylinder for use later, rather than being delivered direct to the taps after heating. From the early 1960s to the late 1980s, when combi boilers arrived, the majority of our homes had indirect systems. Before that period, hot water was often delivered by individual direct water heaters fitted at sinks and basins. The good thing about an indirect system is that the hot water storage cylinder can be sized to suit our needs and heavily lagged with insulation to keep the water hot. You can store enough water to fill a bath or pump to a shower.

Because we tend to use solar heating as part of a combined system, the storage cylinders can be of a pre-heated type or twin coiled so that the solar heated water passes through the lower coil, heating the system water in the upper coil above it. The coil in this system is the heat

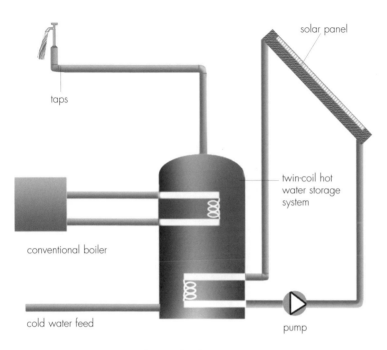

taps

solar panel

twin-coil hot
water storage
system

conventional boiler

cold water feed

pump

Indirect solar hot water system

exchanger. It means that the solar heated water can be mixed with anti-freeze; it circulates around its own loop, passing through the collector panel and cylinder en-route. If you live in a hard water area where lime scale build-up causes damage to your plumbing system and appliances, then this is a better system for you. Its efficiency can be as good as 85 per cent. Since we are much better at storing hot water than we are at storing electricity, solar hot water is far more economical. Even in northern climates, we can produce most, if not all, of our hot water needs in the summer months by solar energy. In the winter, we can reduce our use of gas, oil or electricity for heating water, making savings while we cut down on our home's carbon emissions.

DIRECT HOT WATER SYSTEMS

In a direct system, you don't store the hot water at all, so no cylinder is required. The hot water you produce is available for direct use at the taps, and if you employed only solar panels to provide it, you would only be able to wash when the sun was out. The water passing through the solar panel is the water that comes out of your taps, so you can't add anything to it, such as anti-freeze. It has to remain untainted and potable, fit for cooking and drinking. If you live in Yemen for example, or anywhere blessed with no less than 11 hours of sunshine a day, this could be the system for you.

For the rest of us, a different kind of direct hot water system is available, one that sends the heated water to the taps via

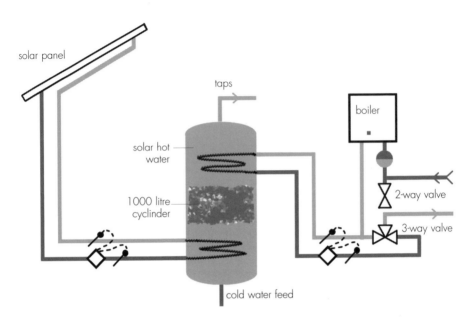

Indirect solar hot water system (showing valves)

a combi boiler or a direct cylinder. Both heat the water coming into our homes before sending it straight to the taps on demand. To achieve this, they have to raise the temperature of the incoming water very quickly, burning a great deal of fuel in the process. In a northern winter, the incoming water supply is very cold, perhaps only 2 or 3°C above freezing, and it needs raising to 60°C in the boiler.

Now you can see the advantage of preheating the water with a solar panel before it hits the boiler. If the water is heated by 20°C by the sun's energy, it will mean less work for the boiler and less burnt fuel. In parts of Europe, combination boilers are designed to accept preheated water, but not everywhere, and that includes the UK. In 2006 it had 'enjoyed' a thriving combi

boiler market for ten years or more, but thriving on the manufacturers' terms. UK combi boilers are unable to cope with a preheated water supply, but hopefully that will change soon.

INTEGRATED HEATING AND HOT WATER SYSTEMS

Most homes where the hot water and heating systems are powered by a boiler can be converted to integrated systems. By 'integrated', I mean a system that uses solar energy whenever it can as a priority, but automatically switches back to the boiler for heat when it can't.

For those thinking of converting to an integrated system, buying a supply and installation package from a reputable specialist company is probably the best solution. The reason is that the package will be in kit form with tested modules that offer guaranteed performance. This modular approach is the key to the success of such kits.

Whether a kit employs a flat-plate or an evacuated-tube collector may depend on the system manufacturer rather than your particular choice, but this downside is balanced by other elements. These systems usually have the ability to intelligently control mixer valves, stop valves and pumps, switching from one heat source to another by themselves. To optimize the use of solar energy, this is essential.

Aside from these units, you will need to find storage space for a twin-coil hot water cylinder, which has the ability to store water in two separate pipes at greatly differing temperatures. These double storage vessels may be described as 'stratifying thermal buffers' in the sales brochure, but whatever you call them, they keep the water at a safe temperature

and reliably available. Like most hot water cylinders today, they are large and capacious to meet our demands, so you do need substantial space to house one. A typical 800 litre cylinder would be 2 m high when plumbed in and, when wrapped in insulation, a good metre in diameter, so it won't fit under the kitchen sink. If you don't have an existing cylinder cupboard that you can convert, and you don't want to lose valuable room space by building one, you may be able to use the loft. That is only a possibility, however, because the solar collector must be significantly higher than the cylinder to feed it from the top. This is because the top is where the hot water from the solar panel or the boiler arrives before it slowly permeates down through the cylinder. Thus the water at the top of the cylinder is the hottest (typically around 50°C), being used to supply the taps; as it sinks and cools to the middle of the tank, it is used for your central heating, which

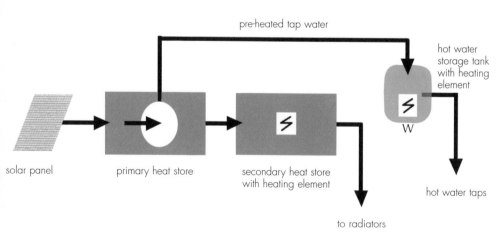

Schematic layout for an integrated heating and hot water system

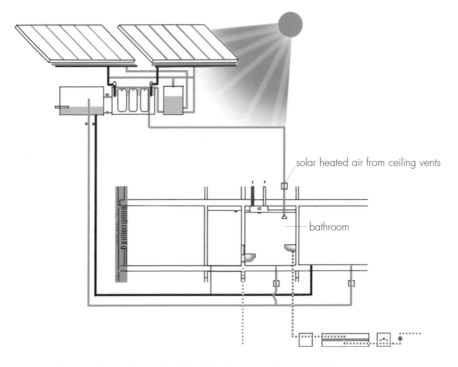

solar heated air from ceiling vents

bathroom

Solar panels can be used with whole house ventilation and heat recovery systems

typically runs a bit cooler at around 40°C. These temperatures are a little lower than a conventional system delivers, because most boilers heat water to 60°C (even though at this temperature, it's too hot to wash with), but in fact these lower temperatures increase the efficiency of the integrated system, making it even more economical to run.

The thermal buffer allows short bursts of heat from your solar collector (when the sun suddenly appears from behind the clouds) to be stored without too much of a loss of temperature. In a standard single-pipe hot water cylinder, if that hot water was added to the warm water in the cylinder, they would mix together and the fresh charge of hot water would lose its heat too quickly. By separating the water in two coils, this doesn't happen.

The other piece of the project you can show off to your friends is the controller. This provides complete control over the system, allowing you to switch from low to high running temperatures as required. Some even record and display the solar energy used so you can check up on how much free heat you've been getting. Like most controllers these days, it can be fitted remotely from the equipment, being mounted on a wall somewhere in your home that suits you. That way you can check the display easily and conveniently.

Integrated systems are unvented and have the advantage of instant hot water at the tap without the mechanical intervention of a short-cycle boiler. If you have a combi boiler at present (known generically as a short-cycling boiler), the wear and tear on it will be reduced dramatically by converting to a solar integrated system because it won't be firing up half as often. I am of the opinion that this reduction in maintenance could represent your biggest saving, never mind the fuel bill.

One of the common complaints householders have about combi boilers is having to open the hot water tap for a while before the hot water actually comes out. When you're filling a basin to wash with for example, you have to leave the plug out, wasting water until its temperature rises sufficiently.

This problem is solved with an integrated system, because the water supply that comes in straight from the cold rising main pipe when you open the taps passes over a heat-exchanger plate, which instantly heats the water. At the same time, hot water from the top of the cylinder is pumped through the other side of the heat exchanger to heat it. Thus the heat is exchanged from one side to the other, and the hot water is delivered instantly to the taps thanks to solar energy. The flow rates from these systems are always much higher than with combi boilers, which at best have to run around 12 litres/min, but typically deliver less than 10 litres/min. With these thermal-store systems, you can choose flow rates from 20 to 50 litres/min depending on your needs. I suspect that you could run a hotel with a dozen showers in en-suites from the highest performing models, so one delivering 20 litres/min will serve most homes nicely.

Like any sealed (unvented) system running under pressure, the installation will include the usual pressure gauge and relief valves as well as a flow gauge. It doesn't matter if the boiler is gas- or oil-fired, or even a wood burner; all can be converted to integrated fuel and use the sun's energy for free. And one day, you will be able to add a wind turbine to the system or indeed any other renewable energy source to help heat your water. They are adaptable.

Integrated systems like this could be installed into many new homes currently under construction if developers had the will, but they can also be retrofitted into existing homes, retaining the existing boiler and much of the plumbing. You can add more sophisticated controls to suit your budget, such as weather compensators. Take a look at the section on upgrading your controls.

COMPACT SYSTEMS FOR COMPACT HOMES

If you aren't inclined to run to the cost of a fully integrated system that manages all your hot water needs, you could simply consider providing some solar heated water at the taps. After all you might not have enough space to house a full-size storage cylinder. Some solar systems can be much more compact, with slim-line, wall mounted cylinders that fit nicely into small modern homes. Because of this, they are proving popular with social housing suppliers such as housing associations as well as the water regulators.

Such systems still deliver hot water at mains pressure and, depending on how compact you go for, up to around 140 litres of it per day. If your hot water needs match that (four people might not find that sufficient, but two definitely would) and space is tight, this could be the system for you.

Like the larger integrated systems, the cylinder is fed by mains-pressure cold water and heated principally by a solar panel with a conventional boiler or electric heater as a back-up for when the sun isn't doing its job. Although the solution fed through the cylinder is separated from the water supplied to the taps, some of these cylinders employ a drain-back feature, which means that they don't have to circulate a water/anti-freeze solution through the solar panel. Drain-back means that the water flows back from the panel into the cylinder when it is not needed, preventing it from lying dormant in cold pipes or a cold solar panel waiting to freeze in winter. The same gravity drain system avoids the risk of the water overheating (which can also cause damage) in the event of a power cut for example. Because drain-back works by gravity, it is a fail-safe system that only a pipe blockage could disrupt.

The controls are fully integrated with the cylinder and more advanced units may even incorporate a self-diagnostic facility. From their appearance, these units don't look as though they are designed to be hidden away in a cupboard or the attic like the larger cylinders. They are cased and are very similar to a small modern

boiler, and wouldn't look out of place on a kitchen or utility room wall. They do have a reduced capacity and you need to be sure that the one you choose will meet your needs before you install it, and it won't help to heat your home as well. Even so they are much cheaper, require little maintenance and have been in development for at least 20 years in countries like the Netherlands. If your home hasn't got the room for a 2 m high, 1 m wide tank, take a look at the sizes of these systems. Typically half the width and half the depth, they average 500 mm wide and are third less high at 1.4 m. Weight is significantly less at around 200 kg when full of water, but you still need as robust a fixing to a solid wall (not necessarily an external wall) as you would for a combi boiler. The water is heated in a stainless steel double coil inside the cylinder, which itself might contain 120 litres or more. As far as the plumbing goes, two insulated pipes for the supply and return run between the solar collector on the roof and the cylinder; a sensor cable also connects them, making the system quite simple to install.

For the drain-back to work, the cylinder must be lower than the panel. It only needs to be 300 mm or so below it, as long as the pipes have a minimum gradient (fall) of 30 mm over a metre. This makes such systems suitable for single-storey homes, extensions and even loft conversions, where other plumbing installations that involve cold water storage tanks are often difficult, if not impossible, to achieve.

On the negative side, compact systems are not always compatible with combi boilers, and apart from the limited volume of water, the recovery rate after you've drained it is worth looking at because it could be some time before the tank is refilled with hot water. Not ideal if you were having a long shower. My advice is to do some product investigation first and choose the largest tank you can afford to fit in.

Warm air heating

Space heating through hot water circulation might be common in Europe, but in other countries, such as the USA, warm air heating is prevalent. Air can be heated most efficiently by solar panels without much modification to an existing system. If you're converting to a whole-house ventilation system to improve air quality, instead of warming the air with an electric heater, as many of these units do, let a solar collector do the work instead. Advice on whole-house ventilation is given in Chapter 5.

Geothermal heating

Solar roof panels are perfect for heating stored hot water, but they aren't so suitable for space heating our homes, simply because we need our heating the most when the sun isn't shining, during the dark hours and in the grip of winter. But as strange as it may seem, solar energy can still be found at these times, energy that is reliable and constant enough to be used for heating. We find it not from above, but from below – stored in the earth beneath us.

Below the frost penetration level, the temperature of the ground remains more or less stable. In most climates, frost protection is guaranteed at around 0.9-1.5 m below the surface, but the

deeper you go, the more stable the temperature becomes.

Temperatures of between 10 and 20°C can commonly be found at these depths, depending on latitude, and will vary throughout the year by only a few degrees at most. In the air, a temperature range that is far more extreme is common. Even in the temperate south-east of England for

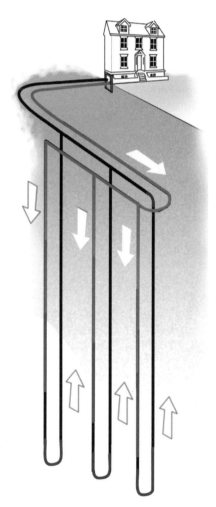

Vertical loop heat exchange system

example, low winter temperatures of -5°C and high summer temperatures of 30°C aren't unusual. Here, the range in air temperatures each month of the year is typically in the order of 20–25°C, but 1 m below the surface, the temperature hardly varies.

If you imagine a wet central heating system, with its circuit of pipes and radiators for hot water circulation, then mentally add some more pipework to it running outside and down into the earth before looping back up into your home, you have an image of a geo-thermal system.

It is rather annoying that the sales brochures for such systems often feature volcanic eruptions, suggesting that somehow your home will be tapping into a lava stream at the earth's core, but that's marketing for you. The technology is embarrassingly simple and was first developed as far back as the 1940s.

In winter heat is drawn out of the ground and transferred to your home to warm it. In summer the excess heat from your home is drawn out and transferred into the ground, cooling the rooms to a comfortable level. This process works effectively in well insulated homes that are not subjected to dramatic heat losses through the structure or excessive solar gains. Modern homes in fact.

HOW GEOTHERMAL SYSTEMS WORK

Because heat always flows from higher temperature zones to colder ones, the process of transferring energy is natural. This rate of heat exchange will always increase with the difference between the temperatures. Pumping a refrigerant liquid through the loop pipe creates two temperature zones – one warm, the other cool – that act as a heat exchanger. The same heat-exchange principal is used in refrigerators and air conditioners to chill air.

It is the efficiency of this heat exchange that makes geothermal systems viable, since it operates with virtually no heat loss, unlike conventional heating methods.

Systems can be divided into two types because of the ground-loop design. This may run vertically deep into the ground or horizontally at a shallower depth. Either way the pipes are continuous with no joints to avoid the risk of leakage. As with solar panels, they can either contain a treated medium containing anti-freeze or pure water, depending on local conditions and the design of the system. The loops are closed: the water circulating through them is not actually consumed; it simply works as a heat exchanger to transfer the energy. Geothermal systems are also known as heat-pump or heat-exchange systems.

If you feel that your home may not be insulated well enough (maybe the walls are solid brick and can't be insulated) to rely on geothermal heating in the depths of winter, a hybrid (or integrated) system might be the answer. A flow boiler can be incorporated into the system to cut-in and boost the water temperature if the thermostat drops too low with the heat exchanger still doing its best. Flow boilers are typically of low output, and since they serve only space heating systems, in this case acting as a back-up, a rated output of between 3 and 9 kW might be all that is required. Typically conventional domestic boilers produce around 20 kW.

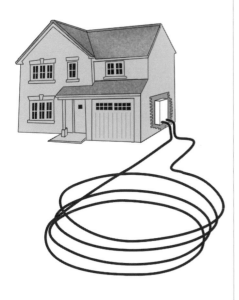

Surface loop heat exchange system

The thermostat could be fitted outdoors rather than inside, so that it monitors the outside air temperature and conditions of frost, switching on the boiler before your home has become too cold inside. In this way, it works like a simple weather compensator control, anticipating a sudden drop in room temperatures before they happen, thus conserving energy by avoiding a dramatic recovery after the room temperature has dropped.

KEY FACTORS IN A SUCCESSFUL GEOTHERMAL INSTALLATION

● Ensure that your home is fully insulated to a high standard before you have the system designed, let alone installed.

● Don't waste money on a vertical-loop installation if you have the land space for a horizontal loop.

● Make sure your radiators are sized correctly for the designed water temperature if you are converting a wet radiator system. They may need to be replaced with larger versions or double-panel models.

● Don't try to meet your hot water needs with a geothermal system if you can install a solar panel. The latter will do this job far more efficiently with a well-insulated and sizeable storage tank.

● As with underfloor heating, make sure the installers pressure test and guarantee the loop pipe work below ground to ensure there are no leaks.

● Use a specialist contractor registered with the International Ground Source Heat Pump Association (IGSHPA).

● Look for a written guarantee that covers the system equipment and the installation as a whole.

● With any geothermal conversion project, it makes sense to design the installation so that it causes the minimum of disruption, but don't make this a priority over the performance of the system.

● The underground loop pipe is often the same as that used for main cold water supplies by water companies and invariably is guaranteed for up to 50 years against deterioration.

HOW MUCH ROOM DO I NEED FOR THE EQUIPMENT?

The heat pump doesn't need a huge amount of space, but an appropriate location for it must be found. As with boilers and other plumbing hardware, a garage is ideal as long as the pipework is well-insulated. A ground-floor utility room or cupboard space could also be used because here the pump can be fitted flush with the floor to avoid any pipework showing. Pumps don't generate huge amounts of heat, and there is no risk of carbon monoxide escaping, as there is with gas- and oil-fired boilers, so a ventilated space isn't necessary.

BENEFITS

- No fuel to burn – only free solar energy.

- No by-products of combustion, such as exhaust fumes, carbon monoxide, etc.

- Low maintenance costs for the pump; often no regular servicing is needed, unlike the high service demands of modern boilers.

- The pump is compact and can be housed in an attic, basement or even a cupboard.

- With air heating of rooms or underfloor heating, geothermal can also provide cooling during the summer for total climate control, replacing expensive air conditioning.

- Ground loops can be installed quickly by specialist contractors, sometimes in a single day.

DRAWBACKS

- High levels of heat aren't available for rapid heating of homes, so the system is better employed running full-time to maintain a permanent, lower comfortable temperature, but bear in mind that the pump is running on electricity!

- Existing radiators may be under-sized and need replacing with larger models.

- If you want to benefit from cooling as well as heating, for total climate control, you may have to convert a wet radiator system to a warm-air system of ducts, similar to a whole-house ventilation system.

- Disturbance of garden for ground loop, particularly a horizontal loop, since trenches have to be dug and backfilled over a long distance.

- Systems aren't always suited to hot water supply beyond space heating.

- In a poorly insulated home, 70 watts of heat per square metre, or more, is often needed to heat it to a comfortable level. This heat requirement could be reduced by improved insulation.

- Borehole vertical-loop systems are dearer than trench-laid horizontal loops.

AIR HEATING WITH GEOTHERMAL

Ducted air systems used in the USA and Canada are easily converted to geothermal, which can replace the traditional air cond-itioning plant bolted to the outside of a home. Install a system of ductwork to circulate the warmed air through your home and also to draw out overheated air for removal. Once again this compares to the whole-house ventilation systems described in Chapter 5. As a climate control system, it keeps humidity to a comfortable level, and temperatures don't fluctuate like they do with conventional heating. The system can be thermostatically controlled by roomstat, preferably a programmable type that can be set and left to its own devices.

Electrical connections need to be checked and air filters changed periodically (about once every five years)

to ensure that the best quality of air is introduced, but that is about as exciting as the maintenance gets. Very different from a conventional wet-radiator-and-boiler system.

UNDERFLOOR HEATING WITH GEOTHERMAL

Underfloor heating is by far the most suitable for a geothermal system; since the whole floor area in a room becomes the radiator, it can be heated to a much lower temperature. Hot water temperatures in these systems are typically between

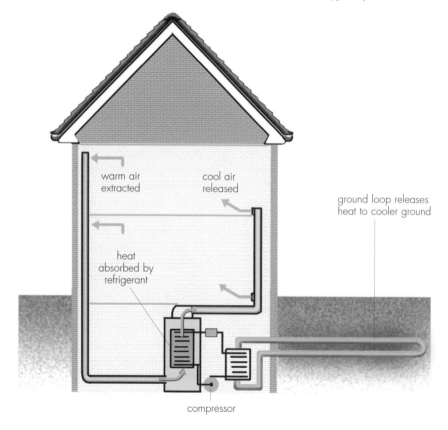

warm air extracted

cool air released

ground loop releases heat to cooler ground

heat absorbed by refrigerant

compressor

Heat exchange system showing cooling function in ventilation heating

35 and 40°C, as opposed to 50–60°C in radiator systems. In fact, there is a limit to the temperature that a geothermal heat pump can generate in a wet heating system – 45°C is possible with a vertical loop, but generally speaking these systems run at lower economical temperatures. Because radiators are relatively small, they have to compensate for their size by pushing out high temperatures, so they have to be fed with very hot water. Consequently converting an existing radiator system to a geothermal supply might lead to an under-heating problem. If radiators aren't big enough, they must be replaced with larger models to increase their surface area.

COOLING YOUR HOME WITH GEOTHERMAL

Unfortunately while air-duct systems are excellent for extracting heat to cool homes, wet radiator systems are not. They may have a minor cooling effect on room temperatures, but they can't extract heat from rooms as easily as they can deliver it.

Unlike a wet radiator system, an underfloor set-up can be used to achieve some cooling of an overheated home, but there is an energy price to pay because an additional electric pump must be installed. In an underfloor system, a water tank can be installed as a buffer ahead of the heat pump when cooling is desired. Space indoors must be found to house the tank, which will reduce the water pressure in the system, even with the extra pump. Also, because cooling takes a lot more effort than heating, an underfloor system would require much more pipework. In a home with large floor areas and low ceilings, it might be worth

it, but otherwise I think there are more effective ways of controlling overheating.

VERTICAL LOOP SYSTEMS

A vertical loop system is ideal for a small garden, since the pipe runs down through the soil, makes a U-turn and returns to the surface, all inside narrow boreholes. The backfilling of these holes around the installed loop is best done with grout, a weak mixture of cement and sand that is pumped in to fill the void. In such an installation the pipework is generally shorter than in a horizontal system, since the ground temperatures at depth are warmer in winter and cooler in summer than those nearer the surface. Anything from 50 to 150 m can be designed. The rigs that are used to bore the holes are similar to those employed in the piling industry, and as with piling it is essential that the contractor understands the geology in your location and knows the positions of any services. Drains, water and gas pipes, and telephone and electricity cables are all at risk of being bored through with disastrous consequences if the wrong position for the loop is selected.

Before work begins, your installer should conduct a thorough desktop and site survey to cover all these issues (a desktop survey will help detect railway tunnels, mine shafts, public sewers, etc, while a site surveys will look for services nearer the surface), but it also pays for you to satisfy yourself that you know where any services run. Installers do offer a surveying service using on-site detectors, but drains are not so easy to locate. The good news is that, in most cases, all the risks will lie within the first 2 or 3 m

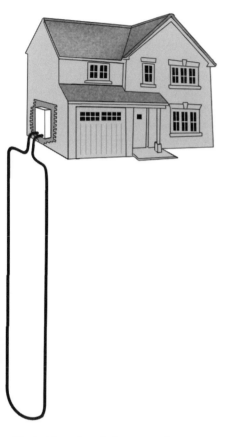

Vertical loop installations extend to over 50 m deep where ground conditions allow

PAYBACK

With geothermal heating, the opportunity exists to reduce your existing fuel bills by up to half, but certainly by a quarter. Not as quick as hot water from a solar roof collector system, but anything from ten to 20 years in a well insulated home is claimed by manufacturers. A system can be cheaper to install than a gas condensing boiler, and it doesn't generate the high maintenance costs common to the latter.

With gas prices increasing, I can see geothermal systems becoming more widespread. Already 100,000 of them are being installed every year in the USA, while Sweden, Holland, Germany, Austria, Denmark and Switzerland have all seen a dramatic increase in their use since 2000. In Switzerland it has been reported that as many as 15 per cent of homes are heated in this way.

Changing to an energy-efficient boiler

If solar power isn't for you, but your old boiler is costing you a fortune to run and parts are getting difficult to obtain, replacing it with the latest in energy-efficient fossil fuel burners means only one thing, installing a condensing boiler. These have become standard, simply because they waste heat less effectively than previous boiler types. A condensing boiler has a built-in heat exchanger that recovers some of what otherwise would be wasted heat and sends it back to the system, rather than discharging it to the outside air, providing greater energy efficiency.

Conventional boilers could lose as much as 40 per cent of the heat they produced. Improvements in design

of subsoil, and these boreholes will go much deeper.

Don't imagine a 50 m piling rig arriving in your garden. Augured boreholes can be dug by adding sections to the bit as it descends and removing them as it comes up. Each section may only be 5 m in length, and the rig may be a simple tripod affair, driven by a generator. This means that it can be set up in a small backyards, as long as it is accessible.

reduced this to below 30 per cent, but now condensing boilers waste very little, perhaps only five per cent. So effective are they at retaining heat that their flues can be made of plastic, since they never become hot. From April 2005, any new boiler sold in the UK for domestic use had to be a condensing type. Unfortunately the technology is being tested by consumers, and the longevity of these boilers is very much under question. Repairing them won't always be an economic option, and many will be replaced in the next few years. Whereas in the past conventional boilers were expected to run happily for 20 years, the new short-cycling types commonly last no more than five.

With a combi boiler, every time a hot water tap is turned on, it has to ignite, raise the water temperature by a huge amount very quickly and pump it to the tap. If you are simply rinsing your hands, no sooner has it got its act together than you turn the tap off. Imagine treating your car like this throughout every day. The wear and tear on the igniters, gas valves and pumps is extreme, and for them to be durable the quality of design and construction would need to be much higher than it is in most combis. I only know of one manufacturer with the confidence in its products to sell after-sales insurance for the consumer to cover against breakdown. Most manufacturers seem to struggle through a one-year guarantee and refuse to deal with complaints afterwards.

Undoubtedly many condensing boilers installed recently will have to be replaced within ten years, because the cost of repairing them and, in particular, replacing

key parts will make it uneconomical to do anything else. Those with stainless steel heat exchangers will fair better, but parts such as pumps and gas valves fail regularly and can also be expensive to replace. Condensing boilers create a condensate that is mildly acidic and quite capable of rusting any metal it contacts; it seems that only stainless steel is resistant to this corrosive effect.

The whole point of using a condensing boiler is efficiency, but it can only be efficient when running to condensate, and that requires the temperature of the flue gases to be at their dew point. With a gas-fired boiler, that is about 51°C. This is much cooler than the temperature many boilers run at. Simply owning one isn't good enough to achieve energy efficiency; you have to run it correctly, otherwise it may not be very efficient at all. The best way to make sure that such a boiler runs in condensate mode is to operate it for longer periods at lower temperatures. You can achieve this by installing a boiler management unit or weather compensator in the system. These are particularly useful in countries where the weather is all over the place and seldom predictable, because the outside temperature is continually monitored and the boiler controlled accordingly. These devices sample the temperature every few seconds and integrate the result with the boiler flow temperature to adjust it accordingly. This means that the flow temperature never runs hotter than necessary. The controls don't stop you from getting hot water if you suddenly decide you need a high flow, but they will reset to a lower level afterwards.

Easy ways to conserve heat in your home

● Maximize passive solar gain – take full advantage of the sun through windows and glazed doors. You can save between ten and 20 per cent of energy by installing south-facing (northern hemisphere; north-facing in southern hemisphere) rooflights and windows that allow some natural heat radiation in during cold weather.

● Install heating system controls to prevent overheating – if your boiler has a simple timer and your living room a simple roomstat for one temperature only, you could upgrade the system by replacing both with a digital programmable thermostat. Most built-in programmers can to be overridden by external remote controls, and it isn't a difficult job for an electrician or heating engineer. Thermostatic programmer controls that combine time programming with regulation of air temperature are much more efficient and flexible. They are connected to most boilers by a two- or three-core wire, and the units themselves run on very low power, often with AA batteries. Mains powered models will have a switch rating of between 1 and 6 amps. The read-out screens tend to be of the LCD type, and some models offer coloured covers to tie in with interior decor. Most importantly you'll need to find one that suits your lifestyle. You can choose between a 24-hour programmer with options on setting each day of the week differently, or one that allows weekends to be controlled separately

TYPICAL HEATING TEMPERATURE SETTINGS THROUGHOUT THE DAY
06.00 – 22°C
08.15 – 15°C
16.15 – 22°C
21.45 – 18°C
23.00 – 14°C

from weekdays. Most offer a number of temperature changes over a 24-hour period to suit your needs. They will allow you to set a temperature of between 10 and 30°C for each of at least six time slots in the day.

A frost setting that will switch on the heating if you're away from home and the room temperature drops to 6°C will also be useful. A programmer occupies no more space on a wall than a light switch, but since it will be monitoring the air temperature from this point, it must be fitted at about head height.

Thermostatic radiator valves

If you haven't already got them fitted to your radiators, thermostatic radiator valves (TRVs) will limit the temperature of each radiator individually to ensure that your whole home isn't heated to the temperature of the room in which the control unit sits. It makes sense to install the controller in the lounge, where you may want to maintain an air temperature of, say, 22°C, but you would probably want to keep the bedrooms a bit cooler. The TRVs on the radiators in these other

Digital thermostatic programmer

rooms can be turned down to achieve this. Most fit to the flow side of the radiator, replacing the standard lockshield valve. TRVs have been around since the 1980s and haven't improved at all since then; they do have to be replaced periodically. If they last ten years, they've done well; luckily they aren't expensive.

Thermal stores and unvented hot water cylinders

For a more efficient delivery of hot water and the opportunity to dispense with those water tanks in the loft, without installing a combi boiler, you could convert to a thermal store. These are large cylinders that provide mains fed hot water without the need for a cold water storage tank in the roof. Water tanks are a problem in winter, being at risk of freezing, and a source of humidity and condensation in

the summer. These are excellent reasons to do away with them. Unlike the indirect heating systems of the past, which heated a hot water cylinder with a coil (rather slowly), these stores are connected directly to the primary heating circuit. The heat is passed directly on to the cold water fed in from the mains by a heat exchanger, and in this way high flow rates can be achieved. A combi boiler typically delivers 10 litres/min, but the flow rate from a thermal store may be twice or three times that. If you have two showers to feed, you will really need the 30 litres/min flow rate.

A thermal store provides hot water on demand, either by firing up itself or by taking heat from a separate boiler. Some can be used to provide space heating water in addition to hot tap water, and in this instance they are referred to as integrated thermal stores. They need a substantial amount of space, but if you can provide this, they are worth considering seriously.

Unvented cylinders are especially good for running showers, given their pressure balance with the mains supply. If incorrectly installed, however, an unvented cylinder has the potential to become a hot-water bomb, so employing a qualified and licensed installer is essential. You have the choice of heating the cylinder directly with an immersion heater, but most are heated indirectly by a boiler. Since they are capable of maintaining the pressure and temperature of the supply even when other taps draw off water, they are often used in preference to combi boilers. Two showers can be fed for example, while a high-pressure mixer shower won't need pumping externally. The major drawback is finding somewhere to house the large-volume tank. Garages and roof spaces are the best options, but you might consider an airing cupboard if you don't actually want to use it for anything else. I have seen one fill a 2 m high larder cupboard in a flat, leaving nowhere for food storage.

Supplement space heating with a log burner

If the focal point in your home has for too long been the TV, and you'd like it to be something, shall we say, more congenial, you might consider a real fire, as long as it's quick to light and clean, and doesn't smoke and smells right? No problem – for the new-age wood stove.

Wood-fired heating is eco-friendly by its very nature, because timber is a renewable resource. While growing, wood absorbs carbon and converts solar energy into growth, and at the end of its life, when decay sets in, the carbon is released. Burning wood for heat will release the same amount of carbon, so you could argue that it is a carbon-neutral fuel. You don't have to go to the forest and chop logs if you don't want to, since wood is also packaged and sold in chips, shavings and pellet form, as well as in manageable sticks, all as by-products of manufacture.

The one thing that has discouraged the use of wood for heating modern homes is the inconvenience of it all, the smoke and the mess from the process. Ceramic stoves and other refractory types, however, allow wood to burn much more quickly and thoroughly due to the high temperatures they reach. In excess of 1200°C is generated, stored and then radiated slowly into the room to heat it over a considerable period. A long flame path allows the maximum transfer of heat from the wood to the heat store contained inside the stove. Instead of allowing heat to escape up the chimney, appliances like this keep it in the room.

A small stove might use only 5 or 6 kg of wood in one firing, and that will burn down over an hour or two. With its heat store absorbing 65 per cent or more of that energy, it can continue to release the warmth gradually all day and into the night. After 12 hours the rated output from it will have dropped to around 0.5 kW, perhaps a quarter of what it was when first fired up, but the fact remains that you can light a wood stove in the morning and heat a room all day. The efficiency of some of these stoves has been measured at over 80 per cent. Of course the ashes have to be removed and disposed of afterwards, and you need somewhere to store the wood, but still these are desirable appliances, being much cheaper to run than an oil- or gas-fired heating system. I'd advise looking for one that uses a balanced flue through an external wall, rather than a chimney. Burning wood can cause resins to collect in flues and chimneys, which can lead to chimney fires, so if you have an existing flue or chimney, it is vitally important that you have it inspected, swept and smoke tested.

If you wanted a stove to heat the whole house, it would need a lot of room and stand 2 m high, but wood stoves are more typically installed as secondary heating systems – a back-up heat source that adds a focal point as well as comfort and eco-friendly warmth to your home.

CHAPTER FOUR

Shelter

Our home is our shelter – not only from the stress of everyday life, but also from the extremes of nature. Most homes do a fine job of sheltering us from the elements – wind, sun, rain and snow – but they aren't very good at distributing warmth or even storing it, and they tend to be pretty bad at cooling down. In hot weather, we often resort to sleeping with the bedroom window open, fitting a giant, slow turning fan to the ceiling or, worst still, plugging in an air conditioning unit. None of these is particularly conducive to restful sleep or energy efficiency.

WHAT DOES OVERHEATING MEAN?

This might seem like a daft question, but overheating is usually defined as beginning at 25 watts/sq.m of floor area, more heat than you wanted. Even if part of the room has its temperature raised by more than this – because of the sun shining through a window, or the lighting – it is said to be overheated. It's essentially uncontrolled heat that might force us to install air conditioning or run extractor fans to cool the room down.

Cooling and warming your home naturally

It is possible to convert your home so that it sheds heat easily when it is overheated, but still stores and distributes heat when needed. A common cause of overheating is solar radiation through windows and conservatories, but unwanted heat can also be generated by electrical equipment such as computers, lighting and heating; home offices can suffer from overheating that isn't caused by sunshine at all.

Crucial to storing heat is thermal insulation; using this wisely can increase the thermal mass of your home, allowing it to hang on to the heat you need when the temperature outside is too cold for comfort. Some homes take a long time to heat up to a desirable level, yet when the heating switches off, they lose heat rapidly and become chilly in a matter of minutes. Before you can install any natural cooling system, you must insulate your home to the best possible standard. A layer of aluminium-foil laminated insulation quilt pinned to the underside of the roof rafters will help prevent heat from radiating down into your home and allow the heat inside it to rise into the attic space, which can act as a heat sink.

SHADING

You can always shade out the sun, but frankly this rarely achieves little more than creating darkness indoors. The heat can radiate through shading material almost without reduction if you aren't careful. Blinds can be fitted to windows, but avoid dark colours and materials that absorb heat. Solar-reflective blinds are lightweight and coated to reflect up to 85 per cent of the sun's heat, but if they hang inside your windows, much of that reflected heat will be trapped by the glazing. It is far better to achieve the shading on the outside of the window by fitting either a retractable sun shade or a fixed brise-soleil. The latter comprises fixed louvres of a durable material, such as timber or aluminium, that are raked upwards at a shallow angle and extend from the wall over the window. The louvres deflect the sun's rays before they strike the glass during the hottest part of the day.

Plants can be used as brise-soleils, but you need patience while they establish themselves. Climbers like Clematis, Wisteria, Passion flower and Ivy can all be trained along wires or trellis above windows. They will need regular pruning to ensure they don't become too invasive and hang below the glass line, but they will do the job very efficiently.

Solar-reflective glass is also an option, but it will cut light transmission quite considerably, so you need to be sure that this won't result in you using artificial lighting to compensate.

AIR COOLING

In Chapter 5 details are given of passive ventilation systems that allow the movement of air through your home to cool it. These release heat through the roof via stacks and vents. Air cooling works all of the time, whether you're at home or not, and creates a climate controlled environment. It could be utilized with water to achieve evaporative cooling, because water is an excellent heat absorber, but only when the humidity

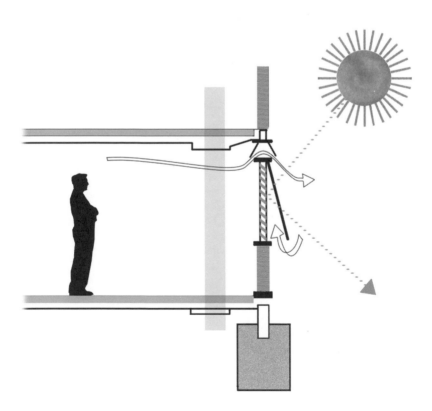

Ventilation and shading can be incorporated in window design

created can be extracted efficiently. Because of the difficulties in achieving this without power consumption, my advice is to employ a different mechanism, an energy store.

Using an energy store

An energy store absorbs excessive heat in your home during the day, preventing overheating and avoiding the need to use air conditioning to maintain a comfortable temperature. Then, at night, when the temperature drops, the heat is released from the store to warm your home and prepare the store for the next day. In warm climates they are an effective alternative to air conditioning, but even in temperate zones, if overheating is a problem, they can be beneficial.

To function effectively, an energy store must be made of materials with a high thermal mass that can absorb heat readily. Indeed, in many homes, it is possible to use the fabric of the structure itself – the walls and solid floors – as the energy store. These are known generically as fabric energy stores, and it may be possible to convert your home to this system.

Concrete is particularly good, but so are stones and bricks. If you've ever walked past a brick wall that faces the sun after a long hot day, you'll have felt the heat radiating from the brickwork.

Wire-mesh boxing contains a natural stone fill energy store

Bricks in cavity walls are only 100 mm thick, and even a solid wall comprising two leaves of bricks is only 215 mm thick, so they aren't quite so effective at holding on to heat as a thicker mass would be. Stone walls are perfect energy stores, which explains why stone buildings never overheat.

If you have a south-facing (northern hemisphere; north-facing in southern hemisphere) conservatory that overheats in the summer, you could install a fabric energy store within it by utilizing the back wall. In most conservatory extensions, the original external wall of the house becomes an internal wall of the conservatory, sometimes being plaster finished, but often left in exposed brickwork. An energy store can be built at the base of this wall, tapering upwards and thickening it, to capture much of the excess heat and cool the room in summer. Concrete isn't the prettiest of materials, so I'd recommend using local stone instead, as long as it isn't limestone, which is white and reflective. The store needs to be at least 150 mm deep, and provided the conservatory has an adequate solid concrete floor that is dry and damp-proofed, building such a store should not cause structural or damp problems. Larger stones should be placed at the bottom and smaller ones near the top, but the wall need only be raised to a height of around 1 m. If you decide to build it higher, it will have to be tied into the existing wall for stability with stainless steel wall ties.

You may have noticed metal cages of stones used as retaining walls alongside motorways and roads in mountainous areas. These are known as gabions.

Miniature versions can be used indoors to build an energy store, although they aren't always considered pretty. You might prefer to build a stone skin, using mortar to bond the stones together, or employ dry stone walling techniques. If you choose the former, lime mortar is by far the most appropriate and will accommodate some movement without cracking. The stone fabric energy store shown in the illustration (see page 88) can be formed to provide a plant shelf in a sun lounge or conservatory.

A concrete floor can also be used as an energy store and can even be cooled by water flowing through a system of plastic pipes cast into the slab. Underfloor heating systems that can be 'reversed' to feed cold water through the floor structure will absorb and carry away unwanted heat in summer. Most of our homes are built with solid concrete ground floors, but we tend to finish them with decorative coverings of wood, carpet or tiles. For the slab to act at a heat store, it needs a bonded covering that allows the heat inside the house to radiate through to the concrete. Any insulation layer must be beneath the concrete slab, encased in a lagged tray, rather than between the concrete and the floorcovering, where it would be isolated. If you are forming a new floor structure as a heat store, with underfloor plumbing, you could add a granolithic screed over the concrete slab. As long as there is enough depth to form the floor screed (a minimum of 75 mm is necessary, but 100 mm is best), you could sandwich a piped water cooling and heating system between the two.

Suitable decorative finishings for energy store floors include:

- Slate tiles

- Clay quarry tiles

- Terracotta tiles

- Non-polished granite tiles

- Dark coloured and bonded linoleum

- Bonded cork (although this is an insulant)

  Unsuitable finishings include:

- Foam-backed or underlaid carpet

- Light coloured polished ceramic tiles

- Light coloured floating laminate or timber flooring on underlay

Eco-friendly materials for home improvements
ECO-LABELLING

We have a situation at present where white household goods have simple ratings of stars or letters to indicate their energy efficiency; the same applies to heating boilers. To date insulation products have only been given an ozone-depletion-potential (ODP) rating, but since they all seem to have achieved a zero ODP, that has become meaningless, and a new system to specify global warming potential (GWP) is coming. It's all a bit confusing to say the least, but it might get worse. Eco-labelling is on the horizon. This is a new science, and it is going to take a while before anyone actually really understands what the labels mean.

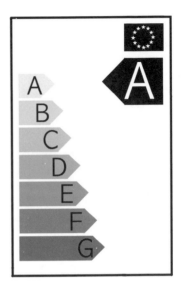

EC energy bandings will also be used on energy certificates, required on all homes for sale or let

When we look at the eco-friendliness of a product, its whole life cycle has to be considered, but the analysis of this cycle often attracts a different description depending on where you live. In Europe it is known as 'eco-labelling', but in North America, the catchy title of 'resource and environmental profile analysis' is attached to it. Whatever the label, it means looking at what happens to a product from beginning to end to determine how much waste is produced and how much carbon is released. This begins with the extraction of the raw materials, followed by the manufacturing process, transport of the finished product, the impact the product has on the environment in use and finally what happens to it when it is of no further use.

Take the humble brick as an example of the life cycle process.

The life cycle of a brick

If you live in Europe, the chances are that your home is built of bricks. If you step outside and take a look at one of them, you might not appreciate that it is currently undergoing stage four of its life cycle – one of five stages it will go through. Hopefully stage four will prove to be the longest of the five, but for all bricks the life cycle begins with its extraction from the earth.

Stage 1 – Extraction

Clay might be the world's most common non-metallic mineral. It is a sedimentary material left over by drying lakes, rivers, seas and retreating glaciers, and it is extracted from pits in the ground. Clay pits have been dug since man began using bricks thousands of years ago, and when a pit becomes exhausted, it often becomes a landfill site for waste disposal; large pits are sometimes filled with water to become wildlife or amenity areas. Many pits are dug on agricultural land, and the act of extracting the clay has an environmental impact. Likewise the energy used in the extraction process is non-renewable, which also has an environmental impact.

Stage 2 – Making the brick

Originally bricks were made by hand, straw being mixed with the clay before it was shaped and left in the sun to bake. Today additional minerals are imported to the manufacturing plant, often from other countries, and mixed with the clay before it is shaped and fired. Firing takes place in large kilns, which usually generate tremendous heat, producing a lot of carbon and air pollution. In fact each brick contains the embodied energy used in a 10 mile car trip. The size of most manufacturing plants is large because of the long tunnel kiln processes and the storage space needed. Chimneys are huge and represent a loss of visual amenity to most locations where they are built. The run-off from the process can also leach into water courses, polluting them.

Stage 3 – Transport

The brick is usually transported by road. Energy is used in loading the truck, carbon emitted in transportation, and pollution caused by nitrogen oxide, etc. The infrastructure of roads leading to the brickworks and the density of traffic often cause disturbance to local communities, and the farther a brick has to travel, the more environmental damage occurs.

Stage 4 – Use

The brick arrives on site, often from a merchant's yard and always by road. Bundled with others, it is handled by fork-lift equipment and laid within beds of cement mortar that has been mechanically mixed, all of which generates carbon emissions, burns energy and generates noise pollution, but the brick finally gets built into a wall.

Stage 5 – Re-use or disposal

Hopefully it will be many years before the brick is dislodged from the wall during demolition. Bricks do have a potentially long life and can last for 200 years or more in the right conditions; most aren't so lucky and become displaced in mid-life. If possible they should be cleaned up and recycled, either as whole or half-bricks that can be laid into a wall again, or broken and crushed to form hardcore for use beneath concrete slabs. Bricks that aren't re-used invariably end up in the ground, where they can remain for ages before breaking down. One clay brick was found beneath the city of Jericho where it had lain for between 9000 and 10,000 years.

In many ways the life cycle of a brick is typical of most building materials, but environmental impacts vary and some can have a direct effect on our health long after they've been installed in our homes. In the following gazetteer of materials, you can see the materials you should choose and those to avoid.

CHOOSING BRICKS

To reduce some of the negative environmental effects that are inherent in brick manufacturing, wherever possible, take the following steps:

• Specify local sources for bricks to reduce the transportation element. Local bricks add a sense of place and context to a home, giving it a sense of place and belonging.

• Specify a mortar mix that is not too hard and includes lime, which will allow the bricks to be removed and cleaned up for re-use some time in the future.

• Buy from brick manufacturers that follow good environmental practice.

• Encourage extraction companies to exploit the potential of abandoned local clay pits as wildlife habitats or eco-friendly amenities.

ECO-FRIENDLY OR NOT? – A GAZETTEER OF MATERIALS

Adhesives

Some of the worst products for directly affecting our health are adhesives, specifically solvent-based glues made from non-renewable sources, like those used to bond carpet tiles and timber in place. As they cure, they give off a gas that can make your eyes stream and give you a lengthy headache. Living or working in a room for hours on end where these solvents are being applied will affect most people's well-being, in some instances, for several days. At the moment we are in an age of resins, when glues are replacing mechanical fixings like nails and screws. There are epoxy resins for repairing broken oak beams and for securing door frames to walls. They certainly have their advantages, but at what cost to our health?

Eco-option – look for water-based adhesives that are derived from renewable sources.

Aggregate

Aggregates are the stone, shingle and shale materials that are dragged from the ground by quarrying on land or dredging the sea bed. We use aggregates in our gardens and to form hard bases beneath our driveways, floor slabs and patios. Gravel and crushed stone is used for bedding in drainage pipes and open channels. Sand is also an aggregate, being mixed with cement to form mortar and concrete. The environmental damage caused by extracting aggregates is considerable, even though some quarries can be converted to reservoirs and valuable wildlife habitats when they've been exhausted.

Eco option – buy recycled aggregates, such as broken bricks from demolished buildings, waste fines (washouts) from concrete mixing plants, waste from collieries and pulverized fuel ash (PFA) from power stations. The last is already being used in the production of lightweight concrete blocks. The re-use of any aggregate is good, but be prepared to clean it (by hand if necessary) to remove any unwanted material.

Aluminium

A good material of low-maintenance, durability and sound strength-to-weight ratio that is used in ironmongery and light fittings. It falls down because of the large amount of energy used in its manufacture. Per tonne of material, it requires a massive 20,169 kWh of energy, six times that of steel.

Eco-option – buy recycled aluminium products that are made from old drink cans. One excellent use for these discarded containers is to turn them into lightweight metal stud partitioning for building screens and internal partitions.

Asphalt

Used as waterproofing for roofs and driveways, asphalt is one of many by-products from the manufacture of petroleum. Consequently it has issues that conflict between re-employing waste and the fact that it is derived from a non-renewable source in the first place.

Eco-option – none.

Blocks

Traditionally known as breeze blocks, lightweight insulating blocks are often made from recycled PFA waste from power stations. Although lighter to transport than other forms of masonry, like all blocks their manufacture consumes a massive amount of energy. Embodied in each block is said to be the same amount of energy that would be consumed on a 30 mile car drive. They can compensate for that in the long-term, however, by helping to insulate the walls of our homes.

Concrete blocks are less eco-friendly than the insulating variety used in walls. They are much stronger, but that makes them heavier and more expensive to transport. Consequently they should be used only where their structural properties are essential and never where thermal insulation is required.

Eco-option – use timber stud framing or recycled aluminium frame construction instead of blocks wherever possible, such as in the inner leaves of cavity walls.

Carpets

Often made from synthetic materials or sometimes from a synthetic/natural wool mix, carpets need considerable amounts of energy in their manufacture. They harbour dust mites, require energy to be expended in vacuum cleaning and are unhygienic in rooms like bathrooms.

Eco-option – use natural timber, cork or linoleum floor coverings that are made from renewable resources. These are also easier to keep clean and more hygienic. Consequently they harbour fewer parasites, such as dust mites, thereby creating a healthier home environment.

Cement and concrete

The production of these much used building products consumes enormous amounts of energy, not only in the extraction of the raw materials, which depletes the resources, but also in the transportation and installation of it into our homes. That said, concrete is very good at holding on to heat and has a high thermal mass, which is valued in 'green' building.

Eco-option – reduce the amount of cement in bricklaying mortar, render and concrete through the use of admixtures as well as precast concrete forms like lintels and steps. These can be relocated in future. Where possible lime should be used as an alternative to cement to provide a natural flexible mortar for bricklaying and plastering.

Ceramic tiles

Covered in Europe by the EC eco-labelling scheme, ceramics contain a lot of embodied energy from their extraction and firing, but they have longevity on their side. They are not easily salvaged for re-use, unless you want to break them for mosaics.

Glass-fibre quilt insulation

A cheap product for insulating our homes, glass-fibre quilt insulation typically pays for itself within six years of installation. Its manufacture does consume energy, however, using non-renewable resources and, most importantly, it represents a risk to your health. Like most fibre-based products, tiny particles of fibre become airborne when it's cut and installed, which can be breathed in. The product also causes skin irritation for most people.

Re-using it isn't an option because of these qualities, and the fact that it collects dust and dirt over the years.

Eco-option – sheep's wool quilt and cellulose are renewable and natural alternatives free of the adverse health risks of glass- and mineral-fibre products. Cellulose is made from recycled paper. Both are hygroscopic, readily absorbing and releasing moisture.

Glass

Glass is beneficial in warming our homes through solar gain. It transmits natural light and radiation from the sun most efficiently if installed in the right position. It is also capable of being recycled, in whole or crushed form. Some insulation products, for example, are made from the recycled glass of smashed car windscreens. The manufacturing process requires a high level of energy unfortunately, but with sealed double-glazed units and heat-reflective coatings, glass can now be made that offers a much improved level of insulation, in fact as good as a clear cavity brick wall. It's unfortunate that much of it is supplied from only a few manufacturing plants and is transported great distances to local merchants. One manufacturer in the UK, for instance, supplies 85 per cent of the country's glass from one location.

Eco-option – select glass products based on their location and orientation in your home. Low-e (see Glossary page 169) coated glass is able to reflect some of the heat back into the room, improving its insulation value. Also consider using the light and heat radiation properties of single glass in a south-facing (northern hemisphere; north-facing in southern hemisphere) conservatory roof in order to capture solar energy.

Lead

As one of the world's most durable and traditional waterproof materials, lead could be considered an eco-option, if it wasn't for the fact that it is a cumulative poison that builds up in the bloodstream to affect mental and physical health and needs to be handled with care. It is used for roof coverings and flashings, and in the past was formed into water pipes. Lead has a tremendous life expectancy; it can be melted down and easily recycled.

Eco-option – none.

Paint

Paints have traditionally included organic solvents that are released through the drying process and are recognized now as health hazards. Other metals such as chromium, lead and cadmium have also been paint ingredients, and although modern paints are lead-free, it is possible to encounter lead-based paints when redecorating older properties. Today's synthetic paints can still cause skin irritation and breathing difficulties for some, and we have a real problem in disposing of old paint.

Eco-option – use natural paints based on linseed oil and turpentine, or synthetic-free water-based paints. Where feasible, leave materials undecorated to enjoy their natural finish.

Plaster

We use huge amounts of plaster and plasterboard in our homes, but the processes of extracting the non-renewable raw material (gypsum) by quarrying, manufacturing it and transporting it make this a product with a huge environmental impact.

Eco-option – natural wood finishes and lime plasters make for more breathable finishes; clay plasters look virtually the same as gypsum, but are far more natural.

Plastics

Most plastics are oil-based products made from non-renewable resources, and many have proved difficult to recycle. HDPE and LDPE (high- and low-density polyethylene respectively) are the principle recyclables at present. These are the food and drink packaging plastics. The world could benefit a lot from recycling more plastic, as to date most of it has been discarded to land-fill, where much of it will stay forever, being non-biodegradable. In homes most plastic products are either non-toxic or low in toxicity. Developing products that can be made from recycled plastic hasn't been easy, but this is a market that hasn't had much raw material before, so hopefully it will develop.

Eco-option – where possible use timber or metal products over plastic if they aren't available in a renewable or recyclable form.

Preservatives

Designed to kill insects and fungi, timber preservatives have traditionally been made from an arsenal of poisonous substances, such as CCA (copper chromated arsenic), a product now banned in many countries.

Eco-option – water-based timber preservatives are available, but using timber in dry and ventilated areas, as well as choosing species that are less prone to attack, can eliminate the need for any preservative at all.

Timber

The world is losing its trees at a rapid rate, and these living organisms were destined to spend their lives absorbing carbon dioxide from the air, which presumably would help reduce the speed of global warming. It is said that football-pitch-sized patches of forest are cut down every two seconds. Often the trees are felled so that farmers can grow crops – not just in the tropics, such as the Amazon rainforest, but also in the northern forests of Russia and Canada, where old-growth forests have been felled for building materials. I doubt that it will be enough simply to slow down this rate of felling; we have to stop it and preferably reverse it by planting more and more trees – effectively reforesting behind agriculture and development. In 1994 some 2,000,000 hardwood doors and windows were installed in the UK alone, many being made from tropical hardwoods cut by uncontrolled logging. The sheer volume of softwood exported for use in garden sheds and fences has also resulted in the deforestation of areas of North America, such as British Columbia.

Eco-option – timber can be a truly sustainable material when it comes from a managed forest. Use only labelled products that have a recognized credential for stewardship. Choosing timber from local managed woodlands reduces the transport effects, but you might also consider employing recycled timber when large-section sizes or less-common species are required. It is a material that can be reshaped and refinished time and again. Timber manufactured into products uses an average of only 435 kWh per tonne of material, compared to 3870 kWh per tonne in steel. The principles of good forest stewardship extend farther than you might at first imagine, and to qualify for it the management of a forest must also be socially beneficial and economically viable as well as environmentally sound. In part that means loggers having clearly defined, documented and legal long-term tenure and rights of use to the land. In addition they must respect the laws and customs of indigenous people in their ownership, use and management of land, maintain the well-being of forest workers as well as protect the biodiversity and fragility of the forest ecosystem. Applications have to be made for certification and they have to be justified. It isn't just about using plantations to recycle trees.

Zinc

This is used in galvanizing to protect steel from rusting, zinc is a valuable product, but toxic waste is produced in manufacture. Although on the list of hazardous metals, it sits well below many others.

Eco-option – use stainless steel for fixings and other outdoor metal products; it will last much longer.

Re-insulating your home

The new eco-friendly insulation products, unlike boilers, will last for decades and pay for themselves within a few short years.

LOFT INSULATION

You might think that your home is already insulated sufficiently, but if it was built before 2000, the chances are you could make significant improvements. Even if it was built more recently, the standards and technology for thermal insulation have continually improved, so there is always scope to do more. But before you rush off to the DIY store and add yet another roll of glass-fibre quilt to the stuff already in the loft, let's take a look at the options.

Products like glass wool and mineral fibres, and more recently expanded polyurethane foam boards, have been the standard insulating materials of the world's construction industry. These products might reduce carbon emissions once they are installed, but in their manufacture they have been doing just the opposite. Glass-fibre quilt has been the basic loft insulation product for a few decades now, but as anyone who has had to lay it will tell you, it is bad news for your body. Made by forcing molten glass through a heated screen of holes at high speed, the fibres are thin strands that can be collected and matted into the finished product. These fibres need little encouragement to become airborne and can be inhaled; the slightest contact with your skin is enough to bury them in its pores, causing itching and irritation for days afterwards.

I worked with a colleague in the early 1980s issuing home insulation grants, and we were both prone to climbing into newly lagged lofts. His health deteriorated: frequently he had a cough and he found it hard to breathe, attributing this condition to inhaling glass fibres in the early days before the health risks were understood.

Unequipped with a filter mask or protective clothing, he told me of the times when he had received a face full of quilt as it dropped from the loft hatch he was opening. Even without direct contact with the quilt, the air quality in insulated attics warrants wearing a fine filter mask at all times.

In spite of these dangers, glass- and mineral-fibre quilts have been considered to be 'greener' than polyurethane boards because they contain less embodied energy than the latter petroleum-based insulation products. The rigid polyurethane and phenolic foam sheets are cleaner to handle, but you still have to cut them to fit, and that is when they turn on you. The fibrous ends produce even finer airborne particles than the glass- and mineral-fibre quilts, and the exposed edges are sharp and capable of cutting your skin as well as irritating it. They usually contain CFCs or HCFCs, and the manufacturing process is far from eco-friendly.

When it comes to re-insulating your home, there are materials to choose from that are not only more eco-friendly, but also more people-friendly. One of these is very clean to handle, being a flexible roll of thin sheets in up to 14 layers of various materials all laminated together and enclosed in aluminium foil. This forms a blanket no more than 25 mm thick that will beef up your existing insulation and also improve the air quality in your attic by preventing the fibres from becoming airborne. Multi-laminate insulation doesn't harbour dust or release particles when cut, which can be done cleanly with scissors without waste, the joints being sealed with aluminium tape. This is a great product for upgrading existing insulation if you don't fancy removing all the old stuff. If you would rather create a warmer environment in the roof, you could also pin the insulation to the underside of the rafters to create a second defence layer against heat loss. If your attic is poorly lagged at the moment, with thin quilt between the ceiling joists, insulating the rafters will keep it much warmer in winter and cooler in summer. Evening out the temperature in the roof will reduce the risk of condensation forming, and provide a warmer and drier environment for any stored belongings. The aluminium foil on the outer faces will also reflect light much better than the roofing felt, making your attic lighting far more effective. There has been a lot of controversy over the thermal performance of some of these products, the manufacturers' claims being called into question, but in my experience they are very effective. You also need to bear in mind that there are a number of similar products on the market of varying thermal performance and price. Those at the lower end of the scale may simply be made of bubble-wrap encased in aluminium foil, but all of them are clean in use. If you'd prefer something less man-made and more natural with very little embodied energy, then your only real choice is to copy nature itself.

INSULATING WITH SHEEP'S WOOL

Visions of knitting your way slowly across the loft space may be grazing in your mind, but that won't be necessary. For insulation, sheep's wool is harvested and manufactured into flexible slabs of fleece,

and I can't think of a more natural and eco-friendly product. It has the same thermal conductivity as the glass- and mineral-fibre insulation materials, but in all other respects it is entirely different. Sheep's wool is hygroscopic, which means that it can absorb water and release it without much effect on its thermal qualities. This is not the case with man-made quilts; if they get wet, they stay wet for a long time and lose their insulation value until they eventually dry out. A mere 4 per cent increase in moisture content reduces the thermal value of glass-fibre by up to 70 per cent. This has always been one of the problems with using mineral fibres as cavity-wall insulation: they are trapped in a cavity behind a thin brick skin, where they are at risk from penetrating rain.

If natural wool becomes wet, an increase in the outside air temperature will heat the wool and release any water vapour trapped within it. This evaporation process may even have a cooling effect on the home below in hot weather. As well as releasing moisture in warm weather, it absorbs it in cold weather and, in so doing, gives off some energy in the form of heat. It's a subtle effect that you notice when you wear woollen clothes, but not one that will be obvious in your home.

For sheep's wool to be used, it has to be cleaned, air layered and bonded, but this process of manufacture still uses much less embodied energy (about 136 MJ/cu.m) than that employed in making other insulation materials. Indeed the process is claimed to use only 14 per cent of the energy expended in making glass-fibre quilt, and it is seven times quicker because of this. The material

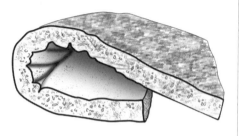

Sheep's wool thermal quilt

can't be totally pure, however, since additives must be incorporated to achieve fire-retardant and insect-resistant properties, but natural derivatives are employed for these, not the usual chemicals. Formaldehyde, permethrin and pyrethroids were all absent from the material I've looked at.

For wool to work to advantage in your roof, you'll need to remove all existing insulation and spread out the fleece in two layers, each at least 100 mm thick, but ideally with the second layer being 150 mm thick and laid in the other direction over the top of the ceiling joists. This will give you a thermal resistance (U-value) of about 0.18 w/sq.m Deg.k in most tile covered pitched roofs.

What I really like about this material is the way you can handle it without having to dress like you're inside a nuclear reactor. The fibres don't irritate your skin, eyes or lungs, and that alone is worth the extra cost. If you're working in your loft, however, with all that dust up there, it still makes sense to wear a mask and gloves.

INSULATING WITH RECYCLED PAPER
Like sheep's wool, this product is hygroscopic and breathable, and its insulation value isn't destroyed by damp like glass- and mineral-fibre. Generically known as cellulose, it can be blown into wall cavities, but also is available in loose form for pouring between ceiling joists in lofts, or as semi-rigid batts (formed by adding a polyolefin binder agent) that can be cut and fitted into position. It has a similar thermal conductivity to glass-fibre and weighs between 30 and 40 kg/cu.m. It can absorb up to 17 per cent of its mass in moisture before this has a detrimental effect on its insulation quality, which makes it ideal for use in damp roof spaces where condensation can occur. You could use it in loose form as an overlay with existing insulation, but I wouldn't advocate this; semi-rigid batts make a lot less mess and won't blow around with the ventilation. Made from recycled paper (often newspapers), the material has borax added for fire and vermin resistance, together with a little water-soluble mineral oil to suppress dust absorption.

CAVITY-WALL INSULATION
The benefits of cavity-wall insulation make it difficult to resist. Since the mid-1980s, most homes will have been built with it already installed, but if your home has hollow external walls, formed by skins of masonry or timber studs, you have the opportunity to reduce heat loss by at least a quarter. How much you save will depend upon the ratio of external wall to floor area, but the potential exists to hit 70 per cent. More typically, in 80 sq.m of external wall, you could prevent 80 tonnes

Six steps to
improved loft insulation

1 Make sure you insulate in two layers: the first between the ceiling joists; the second running over the top of the joists in the other direction.

2 Insulate the loft trap door.

3 Lag water pipes with an approved phenolic foam insulation, making sure it fits snugly together with the joints taped. Don't leave gaps between them. You should also lag the primary hot water pipe from the cylinder, even if it is in a heated part of your home, such as an airing cupboard.

4 Make sure that any vapour barriers installed are on the warm (room) side of the insulation, not the cold side.

5 The loft space will be much colder after being insulated, so check that there is adequate ventilation to prevent condensation from forming. Extra air vents may have to be installed. Tile, eaves and gable-wall vents are all available to improve the ventilation.

6 The attic can be made a warmer, drier space by insulating with multi-laminate blankets pinned to the underside of the sloping rafters, sealing the joints with self-adhesive aluminium tape. Aim for a continuous seal, and use flat-headed galvanized or aluminium nails to pin it up – they won't rust or damage the material.

CAVITY-FILL INSULATION IS IDEAL FOR:

- Homes built prior to 1985 without any insulation in the walls.

- Homes with rendered external walls that act as a rain shield.

- Homes with brick walls in sheltered locations.

- Single-leaf timber- and metal-framed external walls, clad in tiles, render or timber boarding.

of carbon dioxide (over the life of the house) from being released into the atmosphere and the loss of about 35 per cent of the heat from your home.

For those with suitable masonry cavity-walled homes, having holes drilled in the mortar joints and mineral-fibre pumped in takes only two or three hours. The injected insulation expands to fill a good proportion of the cavity and hold in some of that valuable heat. The holes are usually drilled at the junctions of mortar joints and can take off the corners of some bricks, leaving a tell-tale sign that the job has been done, even when the mortar has been repaired. It is subtle, but once you see it, you can recognize it straight away. If you are replastering your home inside or rendering outside, you can inject the cavities first from the

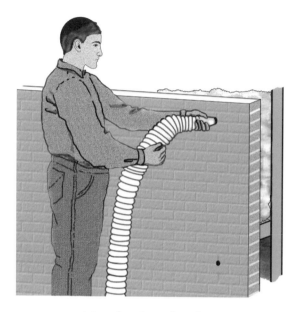

Injected cavity wall insulation

appropriate side and conceal the holes for good. Because of the increasing insulation standards, you might not be able to achieve the same levels of thermal insulation found in a new home, but it could still make a huge difference.

For a while partial-fill insulation boards were built into new homes, leaving residual cavities of only 25 mm. If your home has this construction, you won't be able to fill the remaining cavity with anything. The blown insulation materials need a cavity of at least 50 mm width, and many of those insulation boards needed a residual air cavity to work properly anyway. Filling it could lead to the rain getting through.

As building codes have demanded increasingly higher standards of thermal insulation, all that's changed is the size of the cavity and the insulation put in it.

When cavity-fill first became available, a variety of products was offered, ranging from polystyrene beads to urea-formaldehyde foam and glass-fibre. Like Betamax videos, most became extinct, leaving mineral-fibre as the most common material. Another is available, however, that is more suited to the environment; it is made from recycled newspaper.

CELLULOSE INSULATION
Shredded newspaper is mixed with fire-retardant chemicals to create a pulp that is easily blown into the cavities of walls, where it flows smoothly to fill every gap. In new buildings it is sometimes mixed with water so that it flows better than mineral- or glass-fibre and therefore is likely to create a more continuous layer and better insulation. It

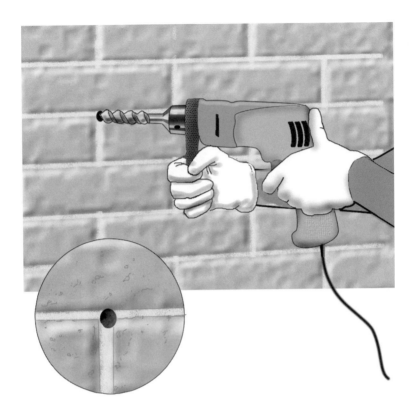

Drill holes should be located in mortar joints

can take a long time to dry out, however – at least several days and possibly up to a year in some situations. Consequently there is a risk of it corroding metal wall ties. As a rule 6–9 litres of water are added to each 13 kg bag, but on-site mixing does present the risk of more water being added by the installers to improve flow. In single-leaf, timber-framed walls, an excessively wet insulation that takes a long time to dry out will cause problems with rot and damage the inner plasterboard finish. In a masonry cavity wall, it should be less of a problem. This means that wet spraying is only suited to new-build situations, where the cavity can remain open long enough for it to dry out. As a remedial insulation measure for your home, cellulose should be installed dry.

PAYBACK

The payback on external-wall insulation is usually good – within ten years – but with a high wall-to-floor-area ratio and grant funding from governments, this can be reduced significantly, perhaps to less than five years.

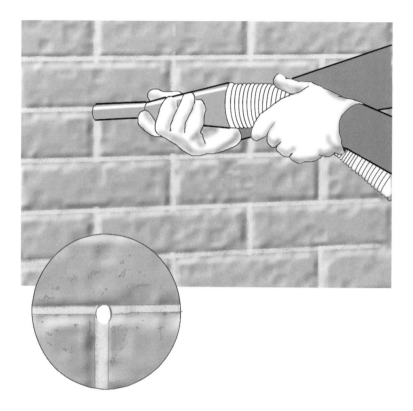

Repair holes with mortar filling after injection

DRAWBACKS

For much of the 20th century, external walls were built with clear cavities, free of insulation, in the belief that the voids would act as rain barriers that would keep buildings dry. Before 1976 it was unheard of to incorporate insulation in such walls, but in the 1980s we started building with the cavities filled with insulation and haven't looked back since.

Clear cavity walls may have become a liability when heating your home, but they will have been doing a good job in keeping out the weather. If the cavities are filled, wind driven rain might find a way through the wall to the inside. If you've lived in your home for a few winters, you probably know which walls are exposed to the worst weather. This will vary not only from house to house, but also wall to wall, depending on the exposure to wind-driven rain. A conveniently placed tree or a neighbouring building can make all the difference. Rendered walls are usually well-protected if the render is in sound condition, but face brickwork is always vulnerable. You can tell when the wall is

A GUIDE TO U-VALUES IN YOUR HOME

External walls

Solid wall	1.60
Pre-1965 cavity wall	1.00
1965–84 cavity wall	0.75
1985–90 cavity wall	0.60
1991–2002 cavity wall	0.45
2002–05 cavity wall	0.35

Roofs

Uninsulated	
100 mm insulation	0.45
150 mm insulation	0.35
200 mm insulation	0.25
100 + 150 mm insulation	0.18

Ground floors

Uninsulated	0.70
Insulated	0.45

Windows

Double glazing	
with 20 mm cavity	2.0
with 12 mm cavity	2.8
with 6 mm cavity	3.3
Single glazing	5. 6

wet because its colour darkens and can stay that way during prolonged wet periods, and therein lies the problem. The insulation manufacturers state that the orientation of the fibres and added water repellents ensure that incoming water runs down the outer face of the insulation instead of penetrating it. They never say where it runs to – weep holes are never installed in the bottoms of the walls to drain them. If insulation does get wet, it stays wet, and only by opening up the cavity and removing it will you solve the problem. In the UK in 1995 the Cavity Insulation Guarantee Agency (CIGA) was launched to provide warranties for such work to cover home-owners against these failures. For a one-off payment, you can buy insurance for 25 years that should see you through a few wet winters. I recommend taking out a warranty on any wall insulation treatment, since the risk of side-effects is always present.

Before installers inject your walls, they are supposed to inspect them to determine their suitability. If the wall construction is unsuitable or the cavities are blocked or contain electrical cables, problems can occur. Electrical cables shouldn't be in the cavity, but if they are and they become encased in insulation, they could overheat and start a fire.

In some homes the cavities were ventilated with airbricks, a practice that has since stopped, but if there are vents serving indoor spaces, they should be sleeved through the cavities. If they aren't, the insulation will block them. Vents may be fitted to provide combustion air for gas appliances, prevent dry rot from occurring beneath wooden floors, and other essential tasks.

Remedial cavity-wall insulation has been established in some countries where cavity-wall construction prevails as a self-regulating industry, the installers having to submit notices to the local authority. These describe the materials to be used and accreditation of an installer as well as the address and date of the work. As the home-owner, you should also obtain information on the volume of material to be used and its type. The work doesn't always attract building control fees or general inspections, all of which means that it is down to you to keep an eye on the contractor.

BENEFITS

● Saves significant heat loss (anything from 25 to 70 per cent).

● Not disruptive beyond the noise of installation.

● Doesn't add anything to the wall thickness.

● Relatively cheap (particularly with grant funding); payback quick.

● Quick to install (2-3 hours).

DRAWBACKS

● May cause damp in exposed brick walls.

● Cavity must be in reasonable condition.

● Minor damage to brickwork caused by drilling and filling holes.

● Requires a particular form of construction with a clear cavity (typically 50-75 mm wide).

● Foam-type insulation and adhesive bonded materials give off fumes.

POINTS TO CHECK

● Make sure that the cavities have been inspected and your home surveyed.

● Check that the cavities are sealed in the loft space – the insulation will blow out otherwise.

● Check that any air bricks, vents or flues are sleeved through the cavities.

● Check that no electrical wiring exists inside the cavity.

● Check that your installer is certified to install the chosen product

● Check that both the installer and the insulation have national accreditation and a free warranty scheme (such as the CIGA scheme in the UK).

Before injection check the cavity is closed at roof level

SOLID-WALL INSULATION, INTERNAL LINING

Without the luxury of a cavity in your home's external walls, you are faced with only two options for improving their insulation: an internal or external lining. The latter is only an option if you plan to replace the existing cladding with a new rendered or clad finish. An internal lining will reduce the room sizes of course, but perhaps not by as much as you'd think. Foil-based multi-laminate insulation materials lend themselves to wall renovation work. They come in rolls of 25 m or more and can be handled safely. To line walls with them, you will have to pin them to timber battens so that they hang in a narrow void behind a boarded finish. Even so the total thickness will not be great. The joints are sealed with aluminium tape, creating a warm envelope for the room that can reduce heat loss through a solid old brick wall to a quarter of its original level. The higher the performance of the material, the higher the cost, but some multi-laminates are not as expensive as you might think and still do an excellent job. Look for the thermal resistance of these products in the manufacturer's data, comparing this with other materials like glass-fibre and polystyrene; you will see that they out-perform them by huge amounts.

In the past plasterboard (drywall) pre-bonded to polyurethane foam sheets has been used for dry-lining solid walls, and while this material remains available, it is not commonly found in domestic situations. The cost has probably driven away many potential users, together with the fact that you need a considerable thickness to achieve a worthwhile result. There is also the problem of creating a soft inner wall, which makes it very difficult to obtain a fixing without a having a cavity behind the boarding to accommodate wall plugs. There are few alternatives to gypsum plasterboard when it comes to lining walls. One is a paper-reinforced version of plasterboard that is far stronger and will take heavy-duty fixings for cupboards and the like. The other is clayboard, a totally natural board that is hygroscopic and made from clay pressed into sheets at least 25 mm thick. At this thickness they have some structural qualities, but weight to match – about 12.5 kg/sq.m. They should be screwed to the wall and, being square-edged, should be given a clay-based plaster skim finish or lime-wash to give the final effect – a rammed-earth finish.

THE UNITS OF THERMAL INSULATION

Thermal conductivity – k-value (a.k.a. the lambda)
The rate at which heat flows through a unit of material.

Thermal resistance – R-value
Measured by dividing the thickness of a material by its k-value (t/k). The higher the value, the better it is. Minimums can be set by building codes.

Thermal transmittance – U-value (W/sq.mK)
A rate at which heat will transmit through an element, such as a wall or a roof. Calculated by 1/R (the reciprocal of the total resistance of an element). The lower the value, the better it is. Maximums can be set by building codes.

Five minor insulation projects
that can make a big difference

1 Fit your letter flap with a nylon-brush draught excluder.

2 Insulate the loft hatch by pinning glass-fibre insulation in a polythene bag to its back, or better still use a rigid insulation batt. Avoid any material that sheds fibres when moved; you don't want to be inhaling them whenever you open the hatch.

3 Fit draught seals to external doors and windows.

4 If replacement PVC-u windows have been fitted, check that the hinges and seals continue to close the opening lights tightly. They do need maintenance and replacement parts from time to time. Badly fitted windows may have suffered distortion during the installation, resulting in a poorly sealed frame.

5 Check that all insulation is fitted in continuous runs to the loft-space pipework and also to the first metre of hot-water pipe emerging from the hot-water storage cylinder.

BENEFITS OF INTERNAL INSULATION
● Ideal in older homes with solid walls.

● Ideal for treating individual rooms.

● Ideal for heating rooms quickly.

● Ideal for reducing condensation by creating a warm, dry surface in a heated room.

DRAWBACKS OF INTERNAL INSULATION
● Skirtings, covings, rails, light switches, sockets and radiators all need refixing.

● Room size is slightly reduced.

● Disruption to your living space.

POINTS TO CHECK
● Face of wall should be well-sealed.

● A vapour barrier (eg. polythene) is essential behind the plasterboard.

● Insulation needs sealing around all the service entries and joints with approved tape.

● Make sure the insulation lining and the plasterboarding are turned into the reveals and soffits of window and door openings.

SOLID-WALL INSULATION, EXTERNAL LINING
If your renovation work includes recladding parts of your home outside, you could explore the possibility of insulating behind the cladding. Even rendered walls can incorporate insulation sheeting, but it is better suited to tile-hung and boarded walls. Along with the usual polyurethane foam sheets comes the 'greener' choice of cellulose insulation

batts and wood-fibre boards. The last comprise softwood chippings (recycled waste from sawmills) that are pulped and soaked in water before being pressed into sheets. Entirely renewable and with no potential for global warming, these woodchip products are not quite as effective in the thermal-resistance department as other materials, but are not as bad as you might think. Thermal conductivity can be around 0.040–0.045 (solid wall insulation, external lining).

In adding external insulation, you can also take the opportunity to improve the air-tightness of your walls with a lining membrane. The latest thin membranes are tear-resistant as well as weather-resistant, but they are also breathable. Some are even formed in layers sandwiching a micro-fibre fleece that will contribute to the insulation. They are ideal for covering the insulation before fixing the cladding.

BENEFITS
- Overcomes thermal bridging through variations in the wall.

- Reduces room temperature variations.

- Internal services, wall fixtures and decor aren't affected.

- Less disruption to your living space.

DRAWBACKS
- The external weatherproof cladding needs to be replaced.

- The wall thickness is increased, recessing windows and door openings, which could lead to drainage problems if they aren't carefully detailed.

- Rainwater goods and plumbing wastes need to be refixed.

POINTS TO CHECK
- Lining and cladding must extend into the window and door reveals.

- Cladding often needs a ventilated cavity between it and the insulation.

- Rendering can only be done in mild, dry weather; it cracks if frost attacks it before fully dry.

- Choosing a light coloured finish for rendering will help to reflect heat in summer.

Redecorating
PAINTING
Most modern paints are synthetic, being made from petro-chemical derivatives. By far the worst element in them is the solvent that keeps them fluid. Until the paint dries, the solvent is released into the air, which accounts for the smell associated with fresh paint. Apart from the headaches and nausea you can experience if you spend a lot of time in a freshly painted room, you might not be keen on the idea that the fumes are often considered to contain carcinogenic elements. Known as volatile organic compounds (VOCs), these are found in high levels in solvent-based paints, but less so in water-based ones – look for the labelling on the tin that indicates that they contribute towards atmospheric pollution, but fails to mention any possible health risk. You may also find medium-, low- and minimal-VOC-content labels, but seldom VOC-free ones. Water-based emulsions are

often low-VOC rated paints, but that doesn't make them eco-friendly. Several components of these paints continue to evaporate for a long time after you've finished painting. Vinyl resins, for example, can have a damaging effect on your lungs, liver and blood, and the plastic binder in vinyl paints can become statically charged and attract dust, which can cause problems for asthma sufferers.

Synthetic paints also have a reputation for creating large quantities of toxic waste in their manufacture. Ten times the volume in waste to the end product is not uncommon.

So what are the alternatives to spreading a synthetic petro-chemical coating over the walls of your home?

NATURAL PAINT

Paint can be made up of just four basic elements: a binder to keep it together, a pigment to colour it, a solvent to keep it fluid and a drying agent. Since it is possible to find natural ingredients for each of these tasks, natural paints are available. Manufacturers have tended to add lots of other chemicals to synthetic paints, like stabilizers and preservatives, which aren't essential.

In natural paint the binder is usually linseed oil, which is made from crushed flax seeds. The resins, like the oils, are plant-based. Tree resins provide protection from insect and fungal attack, keeping the wood nourished, so natural paints can be absorbed by wood substrates to their advantage. The solvent element is provided by balsamic turpentine, distilled from the sap of pine trees. 'Turps' was always used in paint until it was replaced by white spirit, because the latter could

be produced more cheaply. White spirit (a petro-chemical by-product) contains some nasty substances, including toluene and xylene, which are believed to be carcinogens. An alternative to turpentine is derived from citrus fruit and known as d-limonene. The peel of oranges and lemons is pressed to extract the oil; it smells so much better than white spirit when you're painting and when you're trying to relax afterwards.

Pigments are found in nature too, although generally they are earthy colours – yellows, browns and reds are produced from ochre, umber and sienna, but some can be heated up to produce different colours. Lime-wash is excellent for painting internal walls. Admittedly it is extracted from the ground, like gypsum, but as a by-product of quarrying limestone. Kiln baked to around 1000°C, lime is bagged up as powder or sold premixed as putty. It has been making a bit of a comeback in interiors, but you may still have to buy it from a specialist supplier who stocks materials for conservation work. By mixing lime putty with water, you can obtain a good lime-wash that can be coloured with the addition of pigment for painting inside walls. Existing lime rendered walls can only be treated with lime-wash if they don't have a heavy build-up of coatings and haven't been over-painted with modern paints. Outdoors it doesn't bond at all well to cement render, and it isn't that durable – you would expect to have to repaint a wall perhaps every year or two. Clay, sand and chalk can also be used in natural paint to make it more durable or provide texture and filling properties.

For outdoor use, micro-porous natural

paints allow the coating to breathe, preventing condensation and rot from forming in the material beneath. Such paints don't peel and flake off like the old gloss paints; instead they wear out. You'll have to redecorate with micro-porous paint almost as frequently, but it will protect the wood beneath far better.

Natural floor finishes

There has been a growing trend towards natural floor finishes in recent years, mainly wood flooring and stone tiling. I'm a fan of both, but there are other possibilities, particularly where softer finishes are required, that have a bit more warmth to them.

CORK

Cork is species of oak that is different from any other. It is soft and has unique attributes that other woods don't possess. Popular for wall tiling in the 1970s, cork has been out of fashion ever since, but it could make a comeback in flooring. Why? Because it is soft, warm and quiet – in fact everything that carpet offers without the bugs. It is the only natural product you can lay on a floor that has inherent sound insulation against footfalls. Environmentally cork is a good choice, as it can be harvested without felling the tree, and only once the tree has reached maturity. Things grow slowly in the Mediterranean region, where cork trees live, and they don't reach maturity until they are 30 years old. They give up their bark easily at that stage, and a decade later will have regrown to be stripped again.

Today cork flooring is produced like tongued-and-grooved jointed laminate,

about 10–12 mm thick for glue-less joints in pieces around 1 m long. To my mind it is ideal for rooms where carpet isn't wanted, and the noise and hardness of wood isn't ideal. It doesn't shrink or suffer from the moisture-absorption problems of other woods. Children's bedrooms are perfect for cork flooring, which provides enough of a cushion to break a fall while being clean and hygienic.

After cork has been laid, it should be rolled several times in different directions. This is an important part of the laying process, as pressure is required across the whole surface to stick it down firmly. Then it needs to be left for at least 24 hours without being walked on to allow the adhesive to set properly.

Cork can be kept clean by sealing it or using hardwood cleaning products that don't require the use of water. Because it absorbs water so effectively, too much moisture will cause it to swell up at the joints. I wouldn't use it in a kitchen or bathroom, even with a polyurethane sealant. It can also be sealed with hard wax oil or even varnished for extra protection. Use oils that are derived from natural plant extracts, as they may be suitable for allergy sufferers and asthmatics. Cork does have its drawbacks. For one thing you pretty much have to like the colour beige; for another it isn't cheap; and if you're not careful, the whole floor can look like a large pinboard.

LEATHER FLOORING

Although I haven't yet been in a room with a leather floor, that could be about to change. Floor tiles made from recycled leather can be quite economic while appearing a bit on the luxurious side, especially if they are continued on to a wall. Leather is a resilient material, but it needs waxing once every three months to maintain water resistance. Three coats of beeswax, each allowed to dry before being buffed up, will seal the finish once the tiles have been allowed to settle. The material does need to acclimatize before it is laid, and a moderate temperature should be maintained. Like vinyl tiles and cork, leather should be rolled to remove any bubbles beneath the tiles, which should be stuck down with a suitable water-based adhesive. Leather isn't suited to areas where it might get wet – it's like cork in this respect. It is ideal for bedrooms, but given the extra maintenance it needs, you'll have to really be fond of it.

NATURAL CARPETS AND RUGS

You might not think so, given the high profile of pure new wool carpeting, but a natural pure wool carpet is a rare thing. We have settled for cheaper synthetic carpets, while those that contain wool (as a sign of quality) also feature such elements as synthetic chemical dyes and additives like pyrethroids. These nerve damaging chemicals have been banned in carpet manufacture in the USA. The carpet backing may also be less than natural, often being made of synthetic latex laced with anti-ageing chemicals, including styrene. Styrene is the source of the 'new carpet' smell that many of us like, but perhaps would appreciate less if we knew that this ingredient of the vulcanizing agent had been linked to cancer.

A truly pure wool carpet would need a natural (biodegradable) latex, wool or jute backing, not a synthetic one. The wool would have to be coloured with natural dyes and woven on to a base textile of linen and cotton. It would be hygroscopic – able to absorb moisture and release it – with the lanolin present in the wool. It would also be naturally anti-static – you would never be able to charge yourself up on a pure wool carpet and get a shock when you reached for a door handle or a friend's hand.

Aside from wool, sisal and coconut coir are available in rugs and carpets. These are extremely hard-wearing, and I'm hesitant about describing them as soft coverings. In truth they are coarse and really only suited to areas exposed to heavy foot traffic, like entrance halls. As some are designed to be glued down, you might prefer to find one of sufficient thickness that it can be used with double-sided carpet tape instead. Assuming that you'll want to take it up one day.

There is a vast range of natural (and recycled) underlay products, made from compressed wood fibre and the like, that offer excellent resistance to sound transmission. Most desirable if you live in an apartment.

HARD FLOOR COVERINGS

I'd have gone off laminate flooring even if I hadn't seen so much of it since the 1990s. As wonderful as it is to keep clean and hygienic, it is a bonded mixture of formaldehyde-laced MDF with a plastic finish printed to look like wood.

Funnily enough wood is the only thing that really looks like wood. Because it is natural, it is less than perfect – the colour varies along with the grain, which is one of its attractions. Dozens of species are suitable for floor covering, being supplied as boards that are usually at least 11 mm thick. I've recently laid a solid oak floor in small boards that had been machined with tongued-and-grooved edges with rebates to house metal clips in the underside, obviating the need for glue to lock them together. The honey coloured oak gives a visual warmth to the floor that is a joy to see under any light.

Wood is infinite in variety because every batch is unique. You will have to spend some time sorting it before you lay the boards – not to match the grain, which would be disastrous, but to blend the colour. You don't want a tiled effect with blocks of lighter wood against blocks of darker; it looks better if you make gradual transitions of colour and shade.

Make sure the timber is from a sustainable source and has avoided contact with pesticides. Natural finishes of beeswax, linseed or tung oil can be applied regularly to unfinished boards to keep the pores open and the wood breathing. Prefinished boards may simply need wiping with a damp cloth to clean them. Untreated wood floors can actually absorb VOCs and toxins in the air, rather than give them off.

An underlay fleece of jute or compressed woodchip boarding (if you can afford the extra thickness) is the 'green' alternative to phenolic foam.

It is very important to acclimatize wood in the room where it is to be laid for some weeks before doing so. The last chestnut floor I saw had arrived on site kiln-dried, but was laid straight away in a newly built home that was still filled with the humidity of freshly plastered walls. Every board curled up, creating a sea-like surface of waves across the floor.

You might need to choose a species that offers hardness as well as attractive appearance. The Brinell test has given timber floors a higher number to match increased hardness. Ash and oak are near the top end, while coming down the scale in order are European beech, maple, hornbeam and horse chestnut, which has a fine texture and is quite soft for wood.

BAMBOO FLOORING

Right at the top of the hardness scale, above ash and oak, is bamboo. In fact this is not a wood, but a grass plant. Not long ago bamboo was only being used in commercial properties, like restaurants, where a super-hard, attractive finish was required. Now, however, it is popular everywhere. It offers the most resilient surface you can achieve in this market. You do need to be careful when buying bamboo, because most will have been bonded together with formaldehyde-based resins and generate a high level of VOC emissions as a result.

Look for formaldehyde-free material that has been harvested from sustainable sources. Since bamboo grows on a 3–5-year cycle, and because all bamboos die after flowering and producing seed, it isn't difficult for growers to manage harvesting. In the wild at least half the species are endangered, so make sure that cultivated plants have been used. Most of it comes from Pacific Rim countries like Vietnam and China. Once cut it is sliced into strips, boiled in water with preservative and then pressed flat into layers before being kiln dried. Boards are available with backings that may comprise other wood products.

Bamboo makes the perfect hard-wearing and attractive floor for reception rooms. In some cases, it may be offered with a structural warranty that exceeds the serviceable lifespan of most carpets and other floor coverings.

Redecorating your home with natural and sustainable materials will help reduce the impact you have on the environment. It will also have another effect – it will improve the air quality inside your home, and that will benefit everyone who is welcomed in to enjoy it.

CHAPTER FIVE

Air

Indoor air pollution

A fact that is hard to grasp is this: the air inside our homes is more polluted than the air outside on the street. It has been said that, on average, it is four times more polluted. If you can stop choking for a moment and think about it, that isn't so surprising. Our homes are draught excluded, almost hermetically sealed, having been designed to prevent the loss of heat. Alas, sealed in with us, are all manner of toxins. The worst of these are carcinogenic and very harmful, while others are simply unpleasant company that may sometimes give us headaches, and feelings of nausea and dizziness. All have one thing in common, however – we brought them indoors with us. Contained within cleaning agents, perfumes and air fresheners, we introduce these unwelcome visitors daily. Some are built into the very fabric of the walls, floors and ceilings, where, unknown to us, they give off noxious fumes in a process called 'off-gassing'. Others we bring in from the outside on our clothes and skin.

We all know about air pollution – smoke, exhaust fumes, the grime of the industrial age. There was a time when you couldn't walk down the road without choking. We cleaned it up and we are continuing to clean it up. Today the air in Europe is cleaner than it's been for centuries, so much so that it has led to a dramatic increase in the amount of ultra-violet (UV) radiation getting to the Earth, accelerating global warming. At the same time, we have been getting better at insulating our homes, draught-proofing them – sealing them up. Indeed in the UK,

as part of our war on carbon emissions, we soon will be pressure testing new homes to prove that developers have built them airtight and free from the unwanted leakage of heated air.

Now our bodies contain traces of 500 chemicals that didn't even exist before 1920. By 2005 Europe's population was losing one person every hour to asthma, a death rate that had increased by 500 per cent since 1995. The increase in sufferers has been even more phenomenal, and children are particularly at risk from the condition. What's causing the increase is unclear, but asthma is an illness caused by a body's immune system going into overdrive.

As this is being written, at the beginning of 2006, the subject of indoor air pollution in our homes has barely been raised. There is no legislation to control it, and we are free to generate as much indoor pollution as we like. Well that's not entirely true – in 1985 a requirement known as D1 entered the Building Regulations in England and Wales, being entitled 'Toxic Substances'. It hasn't been amended since, and it is the thinnest of all the approved guidance documents published. It came into being after somebody pointed out that one of the insulation materials used to lag cavity walls was potentially very damaging to our health, a product known as urea-formaldehyde. Long after its injection into a wall's cavity, it would leach out toxic gas. I believe that it was in schools where the initial concern arose with the realization that young children were particularly at risk to the off-gassing of this toxic substance. You might have though that the British government had opened a can of worms in creating the requirement D1, since it could easily have locked the gate on many of the building materials used today. Instead, 20 years later, it remains unaltered. Many products continue to be used that release toxic gas without our knowledge. Perhaps some people are more at risk than others, more sensitive to the gas's presence. Ailments like sore eyes, a dry throat and lethargy can be attributed to so many causes, even simply the stress of modern life. Despite the fact that the levels to which we are exposed are all very low and judged not to be harmful, the long-term effects are not yet understood.

All we can do at present is to rely on our senses to tell us what affects our good health and what doesn't, and to take whatever steps we can to clean up the air quality indoors. While we may not be able to influence our working or social environments, we can influence your home environment.

A toxic-free, clean-air environment in the home might help asthma and hay-fever sufferers alike; many people I've met have enjoyed the benefits of keeping toxins out of their homes through the choice of natural materials and keeping the air clean with filtered passive ventilation. Our home is a sanctuary from a stressful world, and its air quality is key to our enjoyment of it.

Sick home syndrome

The condition known as sick building syndrome (SBS) has been known for many years. I've spent most of my working life in offices that could be judged to be on the critical list as far as SBS goes – offices with secondary glazing, little insulation, bad lighting, worn synthetic carpets and dysfunctional heating systems; offices where the temperature can be too low to work without wearing a coat in the morning or too hot to work, even with all the windows open, in the afternoon. Usually the walls have been painted beige to add to the feeling of malaise and ill-health. For many years, I have surrounded my desk in a shroud of greenery from giant plants, not, as many have suspected, as camouflage against people arriving with more paperwork (although it has helped enormously), but as a way of surviving in what for me is an unhealthy environment. Plants are great for improving air quality.

Of course we can't always do much to improve our work environment, but we can make sure our homes don't suffer the same fate. Sick home syndrome is hardly ever mentioned, yet it affects so many properties. While the oxygen in them hasn't been depleted, it has been mixed with a variety of pollutants that are inhaled and absorbed by their occupants. The flu-like symptoms of lethargy, congested airways, headaches and dry throats are often attributed to stress or viruses, but often they are simply the effects of living with sick home syndrome.

I'm sure that some of our bad health, at least in winter, comes from the dry air of centrally heated rooms and the lack of ventilation in them when it's too cold to open the windows. Add to this sealed environment the off-gassing of chemicals contained within the structure, our home furnishing and decoration, mix it with the electrical pollution of multiple TVs, entertainment systems and kitchen appliances, and add a daily helping of chemicals to freshen the air and 'clean' the place, and you have all the ingredients for the promotion of ill-health. In this chapter on air quality, we'll discover just how far down the road we have gone to making our homes sick and what we can do to bring them, and ourselves, bouncing back to good health.

The world of volatile organic compounds

In the UK the Building Research Establishment discovered in 1996 that levels of formaldehyde were ten times higher indoors than out. In the world of VOCs, formaldehyde seems to be the dominant species. This vapour is so predominant because it is contained in many products, including insulation foam, wood-based materials like MDF (medium-density fibreboard) and chipboard, carpet adhesive, paint and enamel coated radiators. It is even present in the natural gas with which we cook and heat water. A lot of cleaning products and toiletries contain formaldehyde too. So being this prevalent, you might think it should be totally harmless. Sadly that it isn't the case – formaldehyde is described by environmental authorities as 'a chemical of special concern'. At best it can cause sore throats and flu-like symptoms, then possibly breathing difficulties leading to asthma and bronchitis; at worst it could increase the risk of cancer in nose, lungs and throat. Of course formaldehyde is present in our workplaces just as much as at home, so the only time you might escape from it is out in the fresh air.

DETECTING VOCS

As common as it is, formaldehyde is only one VOC – others are plentiful. In measuring their presence scientists often select around 50 of them to look for. They are gases that do not smell and can't be tasted. In most cases they are locked into our furnishings and fixtures at home waiting to be released at room temperature. The higher the temperature, the greater they off-gas. While VOCs don't smell, in some cases the presence of solvents in paints and adhesives is certainly obvious for days, if not weeks, after application. Recently I spent an hour in a community centre where 200 sq.m of synthetic carpet tiling and some welded vinyl flooring had been glued down several weeks before. The air was still rich with solvent gas, probably including formaldehyde and styrene, and after an hour I was gasping to get out and breathe fresh air.

I believe some internal air sampling meters can detect some VOCs, but finding a 'multi-meter' that will trace them all isn't possible, and results from air sampling are usually taken to laboratories for analysis. So we can't pop down to the local DIY store and pick up a VOC detector.

WHERE ELSE CAN WE FIND VOCS?

● Hydrocarbons are common too, like benzene found in paints, detergents and synthetic fibres, but also in perfume, air fresheners, hairspray, shampoo, fabric conditioner, dishwasher detergents and some soaps – in fact pretty much anything that is a petroleum by-product. Almost all perfumes fall into this category, which explains why some people experience skin irritation and nausea from wearing them.

- Halocarbons like chlorofluorocarbons (CFCs to you and me).

- Hydro fluorocarbons (HFCs).

- Vinyl chlorides such as PVCs are used in windows and plumbing pipes, but also in countless other domestic accessories. These are classified as carcinogenic, and long-term exposure has been linked to liver cancer.

- Trichloroethylene, contained in some paints, adhesives and varnishes. This is also carcinogenic and linked to liver cancer.

- Styrene, in polystyrene insulation, and plastic and vinyl products like floor vinyl and synthetic textiles, is thought to be a carcinogen, but also is linked to disorders of the nervous system if ingested.

- Polychlorinated biphenyls (PCBs) are much publicized, mainly because of their penetration of the oceans through the run-off in herbicides and agricultural pesticides. They have worked their way up the food chain and can be found in large quantities in dolphins and killer whales. Now that they've been banned in the USA and many European countries, we should be seeing much less of them.

SOFT FURNISHINGS

If you could name a store 'VOCs Are Us' or 'VOC World', it would be a soft-furnishings store. All soft furnishings like armchairs are filled with polyester fibres. Since these materials would fuel a rapid fire and release toxic smoke, they have to be treated with fire-retardant chemicals. As if that isn't enough, pesticides are added to the fabrics to resist fleas and the like. The standard three-piece suite is a chemist's dream. Remember that when you next need to buy one.

What alternatives are there? You could look for rattan furniture and hammocks, while leather is the nearest you can get to natural upholstery, but it will need caring for with a natural oil-based cream to keep it supple and in perfect condition. A natural filling like sheep's wool would also be beneficial, but that might be asking too much.

Carpets are not only homes for house mites, dust and your pet's fleas, but also reservoirs for VOCs. Tests carried in the USA have revealed that even 20-year-old carpets were still off-gassing VOCs. New carpets come complete with a flame-retardant known as BDE-209 as well as pesticides like permethrin and tributyltin together with the ever-present formaldehyde. Being gases they float about in the air until we inhale them, but not all of them are able to float so well, and these are often described as being less volatile, waiting to be roused by feet on the carpet or a door slamming.

I've been gradually phasing out carpets in my home in favour of ceramic tiles and floating wood floors. Cork would be an even better natural alternative to carpet if you don't want to increase the sound reverberation (echo effect) in a room; it's soft enough to absorb noise.

So if VOCs can be found everywhere,

Ten ways to
improve the air quality in your home

1 Adopt a window opening routine. Nothing freshens the place more than an open window, except two open windows in opposite walls of a room. The air change will be rapid and effective, and if you aren't in the habit already, get into the routine of airing your home in this way. You can't leave casements open for long, but fanlight windows can sometimes be left open permanently without compromising security. If you open the windows at the front of your home, you'll be able to double-check when you leave that you've closed them all.

2 Fit background trickle vents if you can't leave the windows open and go out, and you don't always want them open when the weather's bad. Trickle vents, which let through a background supply of air, are draught-free when fitted to the heads of windows. They are insect-proof too. You can close them off entirely if you want or leave them fully open. Fitting them requires nothing more than a drill and a screwdriver – 10 mm diameter holes are typically drilled in a line to form a continuous channel in the head of the window frame, then the vents are screwed on inside and out. The outer part contains a weather hood or cowl to keep out the rain. An 800 mm long vent will provide a room with 8000 sq.mm of background ventilation that can be left open without compromising security. If these vents are fitted to opposite windows, they will keep the air flowing across the room.

3 No smoking policy. This is an easy one to follow if you have a non-smoking household; relatives and friends can be invited to smoke outside in the garden (with the door shut). I imagine that dedicated smokers should already be used to enjoying adverse weather conditions and isolation, so won't feel offended.

4 Avoid using bleaches. Bleach is one of the major sources of dioxin, being used along with other toxic detergents for cleaning. Bleaches kill living organisms efficiently, but then so did copper chromated arsenic wood preservative, and now that's banned. Humans are living organisms too and, as such, aren't entirely immune from the effects of such aggressive chemicals. As an alternative try using vegetable-based cleaners that include vinegar, lemon juice and baking soda. These are natural products, and the lemon juice at least smells so much better.

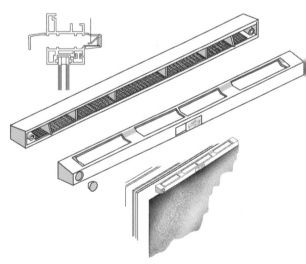

Trickle vent components

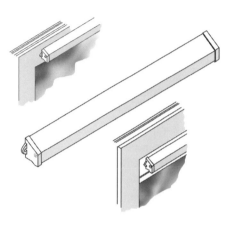

Trickle vents with weathering cowl

7 Avoid aerosol products. Ban aerosols – the gas propelled contents leave a cloud of atomized material in the air to be breathed in. Use pump sprays or roll-on deodorants, for example, instead of sprays.

8 Introduce house plants as air purifiers. Although they are available, thank goodness we haven't reached the point yet where we need air purifiers that pump in pure oxygen. There are more natural means of keeping the balance right in your home – plants. Many species of house plant not only absorb the carbon dioxide we produce and convert it into oxygen – as all plants do – but also extract toxics like formaldehyde from the air. Leafy species such as ivies, dragon plants, philodendrons, bananas, palms and the like are all good at absorbing indoor pollution. It is said that Boston ferns can absorb 1000 mg of formaldehyde per hour.

5 Replace carpets. Although carpets have a warmth about them, they are a great source of indoor pollution. Replacing them with easy-clean hard floor surfaces wherever possible – like floor tiling in kitchens and bathrooms, and glueless solid wood flooring in reception rooms and bedrooms – will improve air quality greatly. Timber can be treated and cleaned with water-based products like tung oil. If you must have carpet somewhere, clean it regularly with a wash and vacuum system, as well as the usual routine vacuuming.

6 Use natural air fresheners only. Avoid artificial air fresheners and toiletries that are based on synthetic fragrances. Natural oils are less damaging to your health and just as effective. Aromatherapy oils, such as eucalyptus, lavender and orange blossom, provide natural and powerful fragrances that can be used to great effect.

9 Go VOC free. Avoid solvent-based paints and glues – look for low-VOC or VOC-free organic paints when decorating. The lack of odour alone should help you sleep, but without the white spirit solvents seeping into your body, you should be able to live headache-free in a freshly decorated room.

10 Increase negative ions with an ionizer. Negative ions can reduce airborne pollutants by colliding with their particles, trasferring the charge to them. This appears to cause the particles of pollution (household dust, pollen etc.) to aggregate together and fall out of the air, cleansing it. This device is effective over a small area, so give some thought to where it should be placed – near your bed or a favourite chair, for example, but be prepared to dust and clean the surfaces around them more regularly. Owning an ionizer is like owning a white sofa – you get to see how much dirt there is around you.

and living without them would prove difficult, if not impossible, what can we do to reduce them in our personal air space and improve our well-being as a result?

What's your poison?

Of all the poisons known to man, arsenic could be said to be the most infamous, being favoured by assassins, 19th-century medical practitioners and novelists. I had made the mistake of thinking that all cases of arsenic poisoning were in the distant past. In fact the largest mass arsenic poisoning of humans ever to have occurred took place near the end of the 20th century in Bangladesh, after millions of tube wells were sunk accidentally into arsenic contaminated groundwater to provide desperately needed drinking water. Even in 2006 around 77 million people are said to be affected by this semi-metallic compound.

Unlike true metals, arsenic can not only contaminate water supplies, but it can also become airborne through the smelting process of tin and copper. Many of us will have come into contact with this poison through the preservative treatment of wood used in our homes and gardens. Copper chromated arsenic (CCA) was the preservative of choice until 2004, when it was banned by the European Union. Some 183 years before this, a popular colour known as Scheele's green copper arsenide was used in paint to decorate wallpaper, and was suspected of causing the death of Napoleon in his island exile. It's believed that in the damp environment, arsenic vapour would have off-gassed into the room. The simple act of handling CCA-treated timber and later bringing your hands to your mouth could cause you to

If you have exposed preservative treated timber in your home, sealing it with a polyurethane varnish would reduce the risk of contamination dramatically. It is more likely, however, that your garden shed or fence will have been treated with an arsenic compound, and if you can't screen these off from contact by planting or with trellis, you should consider replacing them sooner rather than later.

ingest quantities of the poison several hundred times over the safe limit – thought to be as little as 3 micrograms a day for small children. Even low exposure to arsenic can result in headaches, stomach pains and diarrhoea. Continued exposure, even at low levels, may cause cancer because it is one of the few metals that are carcinogenic.

Arsenic is found naturally in many parts of the world, not just in the groundwater of Bangladesh, including the south-western USA, parts of China, South Africa, Argentina, Greece, Hungary and Britain. Indeed the English counties of Devon and Cornwall have some of the highest arsenic levels in the world in their soil. When it was used during the 19th century in medicines, the Cornish mines supplied most of it. Today arsenic is more commonly used in its organic form and is often found in pesticides, such as acetylic acid, disodium methylarsenate (DSMA) and monosodium methylarsenate (MSMA), which are used particularly on cotton. This could be described as the most environmentally-unfriendly of textiles.

Since it is possible to inhale pesticides that contain arsenic while spraying plants, make sure you check out the ingredients of all garden pesticides beforehand, as well as wood preservatives. Avoid arsenic like the plague.

Factories and industrial sites where timber preservatives and pesticides have been employed will usually have a veritable cocktail of poisons left in the soil, and often arsenic will be among them. This soil must be removed before the site is redeveloped, particularly for homes. Indeed metals like arsenic, cadmium and mercury are more often associated with soil contamination and therefore aren't airborne pollutants. In their molecular form, however, they can be found in household dust, and the important quality of toxic metals is that you don't have to be exposed to high levels of them, because once absorbed by your body, they stay and build up in fat tissue.

Electromagnetic field pollution

This last genre of pollutants is very much a by-product of the modern age – an age of electronic technology and demand for electricity to power it. Anything that employs electricity is surrounded by a field of energy, which is part electrical and part magnetic, known as an electro-magnetic field (EMF).

We have surrounded ourselves with EMFs, albeit artificial ones created by our electrical gadgets and appliances and the very power cables that feed them, but that hasn't bothered of us greatly because electromagnetic energy is with us for every minute of the day, not only from these man-made sources, but also from natural ones. The sun would be the biggest of these, but radiation from the Earth's magnetic field also surrounds us; the

geology beneath our feet can concentrate high levels of radiation in some areas too. Light itself is electromagnetic radiation with a wavelength that is visible to the eye. The one difference is that natural EMFs flow like direct current in one direction only, in the case of the earth from the surface out into space (where it does an excellent job in the form of the magnetosphere, which protects us from being blasted off the planet by solar winds), while man-made EMFs tend to be in alternating-current form, flowing back and forth.

Every home contains EMFs, and most of them are low-level. Unfortunately there is a suspicion developing now that in some instances EMFs are high, which may not be so good for our health. The word 'electro-pollution' has entered our language.

The question as to whether even high levels of EMF do us any harm is still being debated. In countries like the UK, where there have been no limitations on how close overhead power supplies may be run to homes and other buildings, this has proved to be a difficult subject. Indeed pylons carrying high-voltage cables that hum continuously are commonplace in gardens, being literally a few metres away from bedroom walls. As I write this in 2005, however, the British Parliament, in response to a Department of Health funded report that concluded there was an 'association' between childhood leukaemia and homes in proximity to high-voltage power lines, is considering introducing legislation (probably through the Building Regulations) that could prevent this in future. Slowly the world is coming around to the idea that living close to high voltage might not be healthy. Indeed, since 2003, there has been a flurry of reports that suggest it isn't, including one notable study in Germany in 2004, which concluded that mobile-phone masts trebled the risk of cancer for people living within 400 m of them, and another in Spain that looked into 'microwave sickness' near such masts. Phone masts are sources of high microwave radiation, with a concentrated focal point that lies some distance from the base of the mast itself. The population seems torn at the moment between wanting total coverage for their mobile phones and not wanting the masts near their homes, schools or workplaces.

Electricity generating stations, pylons and overhead cables are another kettle of fish. With alternating current, the rapid changes of direction in which the current flows and associated higher frequency create a stronger magnetic field. The frequency at which the current is delivered to our homes is considered to be low at 50–60 hertz, and the good news about frequency is that when it is low, the energy is low. High frequencies come with high energy fields that do more harm.

Since these fields only occur around our appliances when they are switched on, we can reduce our exposure to them by programming washing machines, dryers and dishwashers to operate at night or when we are away from home altogether. Like TVs and radios, they have very-low-frequency fields. Microwave cookers, on the other hand, use high frequencies.

So if EMF stands for electromagnetic field, which comprises both electrical and magnetic fields, is one field more harmful than the other? The answer is yes, just as one may be more intense than the other.

ELECTRICAL FIELDS

In most cases the electrical field element is the least likely to be a problem. Measured in volts per metre, electrical fields can be deflected quite easily. Trees in full leaf are very good at doing this, as are brick walls, so little electrical energy penetrates homes from the outside. It is generally considered that electrical fields in excess of 5 volts/m are to be avoided. An electrical field is generated when an appliance is plugged in to complete the circuit; it needn't be switched on and running. Electrical wiring in homes also generates EMFs. Much of Europe employs radial power circuits, which are open-ended. The UK, however, has traditionally favoured ring circuits. Unfortunately these produce higher EMFs.

MAGNETIC FIELDS

Unlike electric fields, magnetic fields are capable of penetrating the solid walls and floors of our homes and indeed most objects. They aren't easily blocked, and some organizations consider that at least 50 per cent of homes in the UK, for example, have higher than desirable magnetic fields within them. The good news is that space separation does apparently help, because the strength of radiation reduces considerably with distance. So don't sit right in front of your TV – it won't be just square eyes that you risk.

I believe that, like most airborne pollutants, the amount of time you are

Ten ways to
reduce exposure to EMFs within your home

1 Where possible position electrical appliances like TVs and computers against external walls so that the EMF isn't generated into an adjoining room. At least leave your mobile phone outside the bedroom if you can't leave it switched off indoors.

2 Replace your cordless phone with a corded one. You don't need the extra radiation waves.

3 Use a laptop computer with an LCD monitor instead of the conventional-screen desktop. As well as saving space, they don't create a magnetic field.

4 Built-in transformers for extra-low-voltage lighting and dimmer switches should be avoided. Not only do they buzz continuously, but they also create EMFs around them.

5 Redecorate electrically affected rooms with EMF-shielding paint if you live near power cables, railway lines or a transformer station. This and planting some trees outside your home will help to reduce the electrical field from them.

6 Consider doing without a microwave oven. If you can't, don't stand in front of it while it's cooking.

7 Crystals are thought by some people to offer protection against small EMFs, such as those around computers, so if you spend all day sitting in front of one, you might want to bear that in mind. Aventurine and lepidolite are both used in the belief that they absorb and clear EMF pollution. They'll also give you something to fiddle with while you're waiting for that web page to appear.

8 Synthetic materials, like nylon, used in carpets and soft furnishings can generate static electricity, unlike natural materials such as wood, ceramics and wool.

9 Most importantly make a conscious effort to reduce the number of electrical appliances you use. Life will go on without hair straighteners and electric tin openers – who knows, it may even be better.

10 If you believe your home is subjected to higher than safe EMF levels, you could redecorate using aluminium-foil coverings beneath linings and wallpaper. In the roof space modern aluminium-foil-encased insulation products are highly recommended (see Chapter 3), as these will also resist EMFs.

exposed to these fields throughout your life will have a significant bearing on whether you come to any harm or not. Life-long low exposure may well be worse than a brief period of high exposure. Unlike electrical fields, magnetic fields are only generated when appliances are switched on.

MEASURING EMFS

It is entirely possible that some people may be more sensitive to EMF pollution than others. If you fancy measuring the EMFs to which you are being exposed, you'll need a gauss meter, which is quite easy to use. You may be able to hire one for a week or so at a reasonable cost, but they are expensive to buy. Look for one that monitors both fields in one unit, as some will only measure one or the other; it may also have an audible alarm as well as a meter needle. Make sure the meter comes with clear instructions on use and comparison levels on what is considered safe. It's important to take background readings and include those in the results as a weighting; any meter needs to be checked and calibrated periodically to ensure it is working accurately.

EMF screening paints are available that contain nickel and are capable of stopping 95 per cent of microwave radiation. These undercoat paints are water-based and low-VOC in nature. They can be over-painted with regular emulsion paint, so you aren't restricted when redecorating. Windows can be dressed with silver plated net curtains or lined curtains that are capable of resisting 98 per cent of radiation if they are fitted carefully.

Remember that these screening measures will reduce incoming radiation, but they will do nothing to stop the radiation generated within your home. Electro-pollution has been blamed for quite a lot of unexplained fatalities, from cot-death to cancers. I have even heard that it may cause an imbalance in the pineal gland that regulates our hormones, leading in particular to the reduction of one hormone known as melatonin. Studies into EMFs for the first time in 2005 were reported to conclude that they could be detrimental to our health. Until more research is done and conclusions are drawn, it may be worth trying to limit exposure to them.

Radon

Of the natural radiation that exists, one form is common to a certain type of geology and radiates from the ground beneath our feet. Known as radon, it is a natural gas that is a by-product of the radioactive decay of certain rocks and soils where uranium is present. It is found in areas where granite occurs in the natural geology. Although radon can't be seen and is odourless, it is a harmful gas; in the USA and the UK, it is recognized as the second biggest cause of lung cancer after smoking tobacco. The gas decays into other radioactive elements that can infest our lungs. Radon is said to be responsible for 21,000 deaths per year in America, and those deaths were expected to have occurred anything between five an 25 years after exposure. Because of this, an action level measured in easy-to-remember picoCuries per litre (pCi/l) of air has been established, at which remedial measures should be carried out. That level may vary from one nation to another, but it is usually around 4 pCi/l. Information on the presence of radon in your area should be available from the local health authority or the environmental health department at your local government office. Maps are produced to show affected areas, although in some cases they can be slightly misleading if readings were picked up in highly localized spots because of something nasty on a landfill site. Remember that radon occurs naturally in the air; it is only a problem when it becomes trapped indoors and is allowed to build up to a much higher level than would be found outside.

Because the gas can be sucked into your home by the difference in air pressure through gaps in the floor slab or boards, radon-proofing can involve sealing the ground floor with a gas-proof membrane. Although this work is disruptive, it is well worth it. Other measures include installing fans as part of a whole-house system to extract the contaminated air and prevent it from building up to a harmful level. This is a particularly useful measure if you have a basement where radon can collect easily over time.

Plug-in monitors are available to sample the air quality and record radon levels in your home. Some have audible alarms that warn you when levels exceed the accepted limits. Cheaper disposable test kits can also be used to make a one-off check.

Air cooling an overheated home

Just as air conditioning has become commonplace in cars worldwide, so it is being installed in homes where it has never be used before. Some systems are fully engineered and installed by professionals; others take the form of portable appliances that you can pick up at the local DIY store. It is a worrying development. In global terms treating an overheated house by burning fossil fuels to cool it is like throwing petrol on a fire. When you realize that many air conditioning units are being marketing as a means of keeping your conservatory cool, you begin to appreciate the madness of it all. Conservatories need shading and ventilating by design to prevent them from overheating.

Air conditioners that are the most effective are those that burn the most electricity, running at around 17,000 btu,

which makes them D-rated appliances in energy-efficiency terms (the halfway mark on the EC energy bandings A to G). Shops selling portable air conditioners do warn customers that purchasing a unit that is too small will cause it to act like a spot cooler.

Evaporative air coolers are those that pull in the hot air from a room with an electrically driven fan and allow it to flow over a tank filled with cold water. In doing so the air is cooled before being forced back into the room. This heat exchange warms the water, which evaporates, raising the humidity level in the room. It is essential, therefore, that the room is well-ventilated, and on a hot day that means the warm air will be constantly replenished. Evaporative cooling is better done naturally in rooms like bathrooms, kitchens and conservatories, where high humidity is not a problem. The larger the water tank, the less frequently you will have to fill it. Admittedly some evaporative coolers come with built-in ionizers and dust filters to help improve air quality, but they also have ice packs or tubes like the stuffed pockets of an overcoat.

Moving down the price scale, we're left with fans that blow air around our homes, making us feel better. Portable or ceiling mounted, they help to circulate the air, but not in an energy-efficient way.

So what are we to do? In my home the upstairs bedrooms overheat in the summer while the ground floor remains much cooler – in winter the reverse happens. Heat rises. It gathers beneath the insulated ceilings of the bedrooms, which makes me wonder why I put lagging between the ceiling joists. In a pitched-roof home like mine, what I could do is lag the sloping underside of the roof instead, which would lead to the loft becoming heated. That would allow the heat to rise through the bedroom ceilings, effectively creating a heat sink.

Furthermore, on a hot summer's day, it is positively sauna-like in my loft. The heat radiating through the tiles is phenomenal, so by insulating with a heat-reflective material fixed along the sloping rafter line, I could bounce back most of that heat, keeping the loft space cooler.

There are two drawbacks to this, but I believe they are minor and addressable. The first is that lining the sloping rafters must be done with a thermally-efficient, multi-layer reflective insulation product – not the glass- or mineral-fibre quilts of the 20th century, which were designed to be laid flat between the ceiling joists. Insulating the roof slope from the underside is not considered to be fully warm-roofing, because the spaces between the rafters remain 'cold'. This could lead to condensation forming within the voids; to prevent this from happening, the spaces will need ventilating. Installing vents in the eaves and near the ridge will allow a cross flow of air that should prevent condensation from forming. If you don't do this, the condensation can cause black-mould to grow on the rafters, leading to wet rot and corrosion of the nails and other fixings. Ventilation of these voids will also help to reduce the temperature between the roof tiles and insulation during hot weather. The cold-void gap can be increased to enable it to be ventilated more effectively, thereby reducing the risk of condensation foming within it, by fixing lengths of

treated timber to the undersides of rafters first, effectively making them deeper. The insulation can be retained more effectively by fixing it with timber battens, driving nails through them and the insulation into the rafters, rather than simply nailing through the insulation alone. Flat-headed aluminium, galvanized or stainless steel nails should be used. The insulation could be stapled in place, but the staples will soon corrode and fail. Joints between sections of insulation are sealed with aluminium tape.

Working from a healthy home

An increasing number of people work from home, and in setting up a home office we have the opportunity to create a far better working environment for ourselves. I think we don't place enough importance on this; it seems to get a bit lost behind the work itself, but our surroundings undoubtedly have an effect on how we feel about our work and how effective we are at doing it.

Separating your home working space from your living space will help not only your mental health, but your physical health too. A room full of computer, printer, fax, photocopier, etc, all generating EMFs, is not an ideal room in which to spend too much time anyway, but if this is unavoidable, then at least keep it separate from your habitable rooms, and take frequent breaks that get you out into the garden or away from it. Converted loft spaces make ideal home work rooms; they are usually rich in daylight and ventilation, and with skylight windows they offer a sense of remoteness from the rest of the home. A garden building that is properly lined inside, insulated, heated and ventilated would be even better. It might not be too hard to upgrade a ready-made shed, but for quality, durability and cost-effectiveness, you can't beat a purpose-made garden building. Even with a shed-like timber frame, it will last at least twice as long and offer much greater weather resistance. Don't forget to seek the necessary planning permission and building regulations (code) approval though. Working from your own garden doesn't exempt you from these controls; there are always limits on what you can build and how you can build it.

Keep electrical equipment to a minimum, if possible isolating it from your personal space. Use a laptop whenever possible instead of a desktop computer, as they use much less power and, consequently, produce a smaller EMF. The space-saving all-in-one machines, which act as printer, copier and fax, will also help to reduce electrical pollution.

Avoid using wireless and mobile phones, instead have a fixed line to your desk. Wireless phones use microwave radio technology just the same as mobiles, albeit over a shorter distance. For wireless phones, most of the microwave emissions, however, are actually generated by the base part of the phone rather than the handset.

You might also take the opportunity to employ safe water-based wood preservatives, lay a natural floor covering and decorate the walls with a VOC-free paint, choosing a colour that elevates your soul, rather than the usual beige. It's enough to make you want to start your own business isn't it?

Improving air quality with better ventilation

For healthy living the air in each room of your home should be changed at least once every hour. This isn't difficult to achieve when the windows or doors are open, but when they are closed, you need to rely on something else – background ventilation. This can be achieved in different ways, but all of them aim to create the necessary air change without creating a draught:

● Trickle ventilation fitted to windows and doors.

● Crack ventilation hinges to window fanlights.

● Passive stack ventilation.

● Whole-house ventilation with optional heat recovery.

● Positive-pressure ventilation with optional heating.

FITTING TRICKLE VENTS

This is by far the cheapest and easiest method of installing background ventilation. These narrow vents with moving slides for opening and closing can be fitted to most windows and doors easily. All that is required is enough frame depth at the head of the window to drill a series of 10 mm holes through it. The vents are wide enough to just cover these holes in a strip that is often about 800 mm long. You may find some that are half this length for small windows. In some timber windows, it may be possible to cut a 10 mm groove along the length of

Roof tile vent

the ventilator to increase the air space. One half of the vent screws to the outside of the frame, and the other to the inside. The outside piece has a louvered cover to keep out the rain and a mesh to keep out bugs; the inside has the adjustable opener.

While timber windows are ideal for these vents, some plastic varieties can be a problem, since they may contain metal reinforcing sections within the frame head. This is a feature of the better-quality PVC-u windows. If in doubt it is best to ask the window manufacturer/installer which trickle vents they recommend for their units.

These vents come in different forms, some of which can even be fitted to the glass if you are reglazing your windows. Aim for at least 8000 sq.mm of vent area for each room. If you have PVC-u windows and can't easily fit vents, you could consider changing the ironmongery instead to achieve crack ventilation.

FITTING CRACK VENTS

Many PVC-u window manufacturers now install crack vents as standard. Such vents are simply double-channel stays that allow the windows to be locked open, or rather slightly ajar. It's a crude, but effective, way of letting in some air, and my only objection is that they might not be very secure. The gap produced is just about the right size to allow insertion of a crowbar for forcing the window open. In full-height casements, they could also create unwanted draughts; all other background vents are fitted above head height to avoid this nuisance. Because of these drawbacks, it makes sense to fit crack vents only to fanlights, or at least upper-floor windows. Most PVC-u and timber windows can be

fitted with a double-stay position to create crack ventilation, but again it would be worthwhile tracing the manufacturer and seeking their advice, even if you didn't end up buying their fittings.

INSTALLING PASSIVE STACK VENTILATION

These systems allow air to circulate naturally through your home by working in harmony with trickle or crack ventilation devices. While these let air in,

Passive stack ventilation system extracting through roof vent

passive stack ventilation (PSV) creates a route for letting it out, thus completing the air-change sequence. The route is built into your home with a series of ducts that run from ceiling outlets in your rooms to a central stack pipe, which discharges through the roof. In cool climates the warm humid air from bathrooms and the like will rise naturally through the stack to vent outside. This air movement through natural convection, which relies on differing air pressure to pull out the stale air, gives the system its name. This is by far the most environmentally-friendly option, since no power is required. You do have to provide an incoming background flow of fresh air, however – through trickle vents fitted to windows and gaps under internal doors. The stack will normally terminate at the apex or ridge of the roof, where a special vent tile is fitted. It is

important that the wind flowing over the vent creates a pressure difference to draw up the air from inside, just as it would smoke from a chimney pot. PSV will not work if the aerodynamics aren't there.

Converting to PSV is a lot easier in single-storey homes, where all the rooms have ceilings directly below the loft. In two- or three-storey homes, you have to find ductwork routes through the upper storeys, which can mean losing room space. It also means lifting floorboards and installing ductwork between joists before you can even think about how to run it up to roof level. Because of this invasive installation process, these systems are more commonly installed in new-build homes or sometimes only to provide part-house ventilation in existing properties. Connecting the kitchen to the system should be your primary aim, since this is

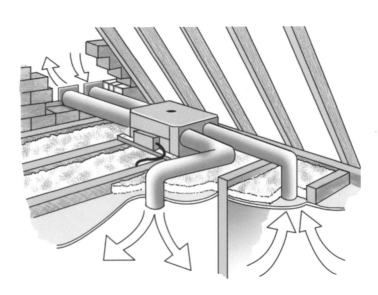

Whole house ventilation system

where the greatest air changes are required. The kitchen is the number-one source of humid, stale air and, of course, lingering cooking smells.

Because PSV systems require a good air flow in and around the home, they tend to be more suited to older properties that aren't sealed up so tightly.

INSTALLING WHOLE-HOUSE VENTILATION WITH OPTIONAL HEAT RECOVERY

This system is the only one that can be installed to provide rapid ventilation, since it incorporates an air extraction facility. Extract ventilation has always been achieved by mechanical extractors that suck out the air, using electric fans that are usually located in kitchens and bathrooms. The vast majority of fans installed are cheap, noisy and unsightly, and they frequently operate when they aren't required because they have been wired up to a light switch, even though the room in question has a window. Extractor fans are fitted in many countries because their installation is required by local building regulations. Their task is to remove humid air from rooms where condensation might otherwise occur, thus preventing the possible growth of black mould and other problems that arise with damp air. However there are much better ways of controlling humidity and removing stale air; whole-house ventilation could be installed instead.

To overcome the potential problems caused by varying external temperatures and air pressure with PSV, a fan is installed in the loft space. This gently pulls the air up into the roof and blows it out. The expelled air might be unwanted, but it often carries heat with it, heat that has cost energy to produce and will require more energy to replace if we simply discharge it to the outside. To protect against such heat loss, whole-house systems are available with a heat-recovery facility that can recycle up to 70 per cent of the heat back into your home. In these, the fan unit incorporates a heat exchanger that draws out the heat as the air passes through. This heat is then used to warm the air being pulled in through a separate air stream and introduced back into your rooms. The result is stale warm air out, fresh warm air in.

Systems like this reduce your energy demand not only by eliminating individual room extractor fans, but also by cutting heat generation.

The warm fresh air is blown through ducts to your choice of rooms, but ideally these would be bedrooms and living space. The system of extracting air would see ducts serving the kitchen, bathrooms and utility room, where high humidity levels are common. The air handling unit installed in the loft is likely to look like a galvanized steel box with connecting pipework radiating from it. Alas most systems consume between 150 and 200 watts to drive the two rotor-type fans – one to extract stale air, the other to pull in fresh air. This power requirement is a major drawback, but it is necessary to complete the air changes and overcome the resistance to air flow within the ductwork. The bigger your home and the longer the ductwork, the greater the resistance to air flow and the higher the power output required from the fan. Air handling units are fairly compact and will occupy less room than

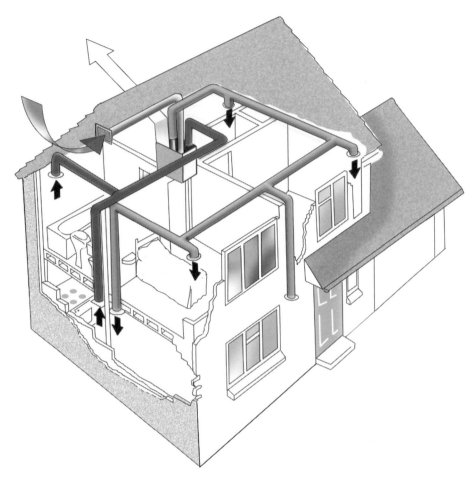

Whole-house ventilation with heat recovery

your Christmas decorations, a box 600 mm square being typical. Along with the power requirement comes some noise generation associated with most mechanical fans, but at around 60 decibels, this isn't too bad. You could always add extra loft insulation beneath the unit to cut down that noise; if I had one in my home, I'd have it fitted over the landing space, not above a bedroom.

I believe some models can be fitted within an acoustically insulated enclosure that is designed for cupboard installation in flats, and it might be worth the extra expense to keep the noise level down.

Because air is introduced by this system as well as extracted, trickle vents are not fitted to windows; in fact your home needs to be well-sealed against air

VENTILATION (LITRES/SEC)	WATTS	AIR FLOW
Background (trickle)	4	12
Medium	8	25
High	17	36
Rapid (boost)	25	54

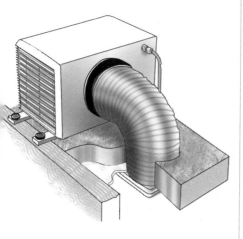

Positive pressure ventilator

house systems more suited to modern homes that are double-glazed and nicely sealed up.

BENEFITS

● Toxics released in the home are drawn out by the continuous air changes.

● You can remove extractor fans from your home.

● You can introduce fresh air without opening windows, so your home remains aired even when you are not there.

● With heat recovery, you can reduce heating bills.

● Hay fever and asthma sufferers benefit from a pollen filtered, clean-air environment.

DRAWBACKS

● The installation in multi-storey homes is difficult and invasive, as it requires two separate ducting systems.

● A considerable amount of power required in most climates to achieve the air changes.

entry from other sources. Imagine how badly your car's air conditioning would work if you had the windows open as well; this system is the same – it needs to work alone to ventilate your home efficiently. When local authorities install these systems to their housing stock, they tend to have the properties air-pressure tested first to ensure that they are airtight. This tends to make whole-

● Pattern staining can occur around extracting ceiling vents where dirty air is removed, requiring more frequent redecoration.

INSTALLING POSITIVE-PRESSURE VENTILATION

A much cheaper and less-intrusive system than passive or whole-house ventilation is one that simply pumps air into your home. Positive-air-pressure systems (PAPs) don't extract air, and again are designed to be installed in the loft. In this case, however, there is just one duct run, to a ceiling vent in one room. It's a good way of improving the air quality in, say, a bedroom if you suffer with respiratory problems or have difficulty sleeping; otherwise it's usual to fit the vent in a general area such as a landing or hallway. Air is drawn into the unit from the outside, filtered and heated if necessary, then pumped into your home. An electronic controller will monitor incoming air temperature and shut the system down when it becomes too warm outside, and heat the air up when it is too cold, maintaining a comfortable temperature indoors.

Unlike whole-house systems, these are energy-efficient; when fitted with extra-voltage DC motors, they may burn only 4 watts in pumping the air in at a low flow rate. Heating it would require extra energy of course, since they use electric elements to achieve this. Alas they don't so much remove stale and humid air as dilute it with clean air, effectively

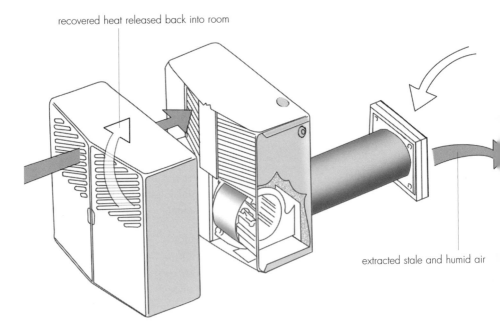

recovered heat released back into room

extracted stale and humid air

Heat recovery extractor fan

'watering down' the pollution. Controls for switching the heater on or off and adjusting the fan speed are usually remotely wired to a convenient place on a wall. If you want to disable the heating element, this is usually possible from the control switch.

BENEFITS

● Systems are quiet running.

● They introduce clean and filtered air without having to open windows.

● Without heating they are low-powered and cheap to run.

● They help to reduce the risk of condensation.

● They improve indoor air quality.

DRAWBACKS

● They don't replace extractor fans in bathrooms and kitchens.

● For more than trickle ventilation, the power consumption goes up.

● Look for a unit that ducts clean air in from outside via a soffit grille at eaves level. Many just use the air inside the loft, which is often superheated in summer, and likely to be contaminated with dust and insulation fibres.

There are some new products that fit into this category. Some take the form of slimline wall panels that claim to use a 'neo plasma purifying system'. Essentially they filter the air with the aim of reducing dust, tobacco smoke and food smells.

Although they vary in appearance, they all do the same thing, so don't become too caught up in the marketing.

UPGRADING YOUR EXTRACTOR FANS

If a whole-house ventilation system isn't for you, you can reduce both the noise and power consumption of your existing extractor fans by exchanging them for more efficient models. I'm afraid builders seldom install more than the cheapest model they can obtain, without a thought to these issues, but you might be able to upgrade them to achieve a dramatic reduction in both.

It is common for a bathroom extractor fan to be operated by the light switch. Even when your bathroom is awash with natural light and you might choose to shower during the day, the fan won't work until you switch on the light. When you pop in to spend a penny at night, it will run relentlessly on a timer for 20 minutes after the light has been switched off and you are back trying to get to sleep again. I can't really explain why they are wired up this way, other than that about 30 years ago, when bathroom fans were only necessary if you didn't have a window you could open for ventilation and you couldn't use the room without switching on the light, the only way of ensuring that a fan was used and the room ventilated was by wiring it to the light.

Things changed 20 years ago when we started installing fans for a different reason, to rapidly extract humid air even if a window was present. Now they come with 'humidistat' switches that only turn the fan on when you actually need it. These new fans are quite clever, incorporating a tiny microprocessor that samples the relative humidity in the air. If there is a sudden rise in the humidity (normally 40–75 per cent), it switches the extractor on. When the water vapour has been extracted and the room's humidity level returns to normal, the fan will switch itself off. Thus you save a lot of wasted electricity by ensuring the fan only runs when necessary. Humidity sensors are so reliable that many of them come with lifetime guarantees. Some models can be overridden by a pull-cord switch if you want to extract smells or smoke, and many run on a low-voltage supply. Some even have night-time settings to stop them from running in the early hours of the morning, even if the humidity level rises. Power-wise the low-voltage fans typically run on 10 watts, producing less than 40 decibels of sound.

Since the vast majority of these fans can be fitted to a 100 mm diameter duct through the ceiling or a wall, it should be relatively easy for a qualified electrician to remove your old model and replace it with something better.

If 10 watts of power is still too much, there are some extra-low-voltage fans that consume less than 3 watts. Being 12 volt DC appliances, they require transformers to cut down the voltage, but these aren't always built in, so you'll need somewhere like a loft to locate them. One advantage of the extra-low-voltage types is that they can be sited very close to the source of humidity, directly over a shower or bath, for example, where normal-voltage fans wouldn't be allowed because of the high risk of electrocution. The closer they are to the source, the more efficient they are at removing humid air.

There is one important issue to consider: every extractor fan has a maximum length of duct with which it can be used. If the ductwork leading to the outside air is too long, the fan won't be able to overcome the resistance to the air flow and it won't work at all. Most extra-low-voltage units work only over short distances of 1 or 2 m from the outside vent, so they are best suited to fitting on external walls because of this.

Personally I think it's worth looking for a fan that has a powered louvre grille on the outside instead of the usual gravity operated types. The latter flap about in the breeze and make a terribly noise in the process. Mechanical louvres act as a backdraught shutter, opening automatically when the fan is activated, but sealing shut when it isn't.

In kitchens the most effective fans are those installed directly over the cooker hob and oven. Unfortunately many hob fans have charcoal filters and simply recirculate the air rather than duct it to the outside. If you have this type, it won't remove condensation at all well. Most hob fans can be converted from recirculation to extraction, and even if your cooker isn't located on an outside wall, ducting can be run invisibly along the tops of wall cupboards and out through the nearest external wall. These fans usually have a choice of speeds, and all of them have manual switching because humidistat sensors tend to become disabled by grease and oil from cooking.

Improving indoor air quality should benefit you almost immediately, while reducing electro-pollution can only be of benefit to our health and longevity.

CHAPTER SIX

Waste

Recycling – the three Rs

The three Rs have been recycled. They never really worked for 'reading, writing and 'rithmetic' anyway, so now we have them reborn as 'reduce, reuse and recycle'. 'Reduce' is perhaps the hardest of the three Rs, because it requires us to ask the question, 'Do I really need that product or can I live without it?' For most of us that's a pretty unfamiliar question. We've been used to buying anything and everything on a whim, and often on a credit card, without really knowing whether we could have borrowed it or made do without having it for a while, or

indeed without having it all.

'Reuse' asks us to pause before we throw something in the bin and consider whether it can be re-employed as something else or repaired perhaps. The last of the three Rs comes up when you have decided to throw something away, asking if it can be recycled?

We are all going to have to get into the habit of considering the three Rs if we aren't going to sink deeper into a world of waste.

The primary materials for recycling

Many of the materials we use in our homes have been mined, extracted from the ground or harvested before being manufactured and bought by us. When we've finished with them, they are discarded in what has always been an 'out of sight, out of mind' manner. We regard our waste as we regard our drainage treatment: if it isn't actually somebody else's responsibility, all we need to know is that it's been removed from our homes and taken away – anywhere. Rather than burying it in the ground or burning it, what we should be doing with much of it is converting it back into useful materials.

RECYCLE

Recycling technology is still in its early days, and new methods to recycle materials like plastics will come in future. Some nations recycle more waste than others. The landfill tax per tonne of waste buried is much higher in some countries than others, but you can't tax people to prevent them from burying their waste if they have no other option. Schemes for recycling have to be developed first, and I'm sure in time that the demand for recycled materials will increase and feed off such schemes. There are some established success stories, however, namely paper and steel. Recycled paper is prolific, but recycling centres have become fussy about the type of paper they accept, much of which ends up as newspaper. If we could recycle even more, say 100,000 tonnes per year, we could save 410 million kWh of energy in making new paper. Steel food cans are 100 per cent recyclable, and with magnetic extraction at waste-disposal centres, they can easily be separated from other waste. France recycles almost half of its steel cans. This is extremely worthwhile, because every tonne of this product saves 1.5 tonnes of raw iron ore from being extracted, 0.5 tonne of coal and 40 per cent of the water used to make new cans.

While it is possible to convert your home with some reclaimed materials, homes built entirely from recycled and salvaged materials are not likely to catch on. Houses that have been built from driftwood and reclaimed corrugated tin sheeting with plywood-clad walls, as laudable as they are, I fear are those that have had the rest of us backing gently away from the 'greenies' while trying to avoid making any sudden moves. In most of the developed world, we are lucky enough to be able to maintain and decorate our homes with design and aesthetics in mind, so converting them into a more eco-friendly state shouldn't destroy that. I am not going to suggest you rip off the concrete roof tiles and replace them with the salvaged roof of an old shed, or remodel the external walls with driftwood; only that you make a point of using products that are either recycled or recyclable.

International logo for recycling

Keep recyclable material out of the general waste bin

WASTE DISPOSAL

The typical household discards about 1.3 tonnes of waste – about the weight of a car – every year, mostly in food waste, cardboard, plastic and paper. A lot of this material could be recycled if we chose to do so. Indeed some countries have been very successful at recovering waste from homes and turning it back into useful products, rather than burying it in the ground, but not all of them. The UK, for example, has been one of the worst, which for a small nation where land is at a high premium is extraordinary. Of course in our consumer-led world, waste is a growing factor, increasing by about four per cent a year.

In the past the fact that half of our waste was biodegradable might have been considered convenient, since we were

139

Percentage element of recycled material

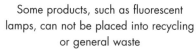

Some products, such as fluorescent lamps, can not be placed into recycling or general waste

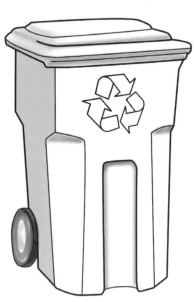

Recycling bins should be large enough to be useful

burying it all in the ground. Now, however, we know that its decomposition in landfill merely adds to greenhouse gases.

Britain is trying to catch up with other countries now and is aiming to recycle or compost at least a third of all household waste by 2015; most of its local authorities have introduced, or plan to introduce, schemes to get everyone involved. Indeed some London boroughs are threatening to prosecute people who don't take part. Separate collections are made for containers of metal, glass and paper, although in 2005 this is new territory and the bins are hopelessly small plastic boxes collected too infrequently, but it's a start. All we have to do now is stop the junk mail from being delivered faster than it can be recycled. I'm sure that recycling centres will be much more localized in the future, and waste will be delivered to them more frequently. Information on where they are and what they take also needs to be improved dramatically, and local authorities need to provide larger bins to cope.

It's nothing to be proud of, but my county, like most in the UK, only started recycling plastic and garden waste in 2004, even though paper, bottles and cans had been recycled for years before. To be fair plastic only represents about eight per cent of our garbage, but it has the dubious reputation of staying in the ground forever. Indeed some plastics that have been purposely designed to resist ageing are expected to last for millennia. They even line landfill sites with them because of their longevity.

RECYCLED MATERIALS AND RECYCLED-CONTENT MATERIALS

For something to be labelled as a recycled product or material, it must be made completely from recycled ingredients. For it to be labelled as a recycled-content product, it need only contain a proportion of recycled material, which could be very low indeed compared to the new materials used in its manufacture. For this reason alone, it is worth understanding the difference. I suppose we have to appreciate that many products we use in our homes can't be recycled. Some plastics are classic examples: while it is possible to buy certain plastics that are pure recycled material, most have an element of new plastic added to achieve the desired result.

Low-density polyethylene (LDPE) is quite a good plastic to recycle because it can be reformed into sheets from as little as 1 mm thick to as much as 18 mm thick. Its brother, high-density polyethylene (HDPE) has a similar ability, but is recycled into boards, typically between 2 and 6 mm thick, that can be either smooth-faced or embossed with a patterned surface. As well as this kind of pure plastic sheeting, composite boards are made from it and used in interior design. They comprise wood chippings, sawdust and HDPE plastic compressed and moulded into sheets. The ingredients may be extended, but if they are all waste products, the end result can be declared 'recycled'.

Most of the plastic collected at my regional recycling plant takes the form of empty drinks bottles. These are usually made of HDPE (check the bottom where it is normally embossed). Rinsed out with the caps removed, these make for sound recycling. Plastic bottles could be recycled into many things, from fleece jackets to carpets. It takes only 25 bottles to make the linen for one jacket.

I can't help thinking that the supply of plastics for recycling might outstrip the demand at present, because we could do a lot more to manufacture essential materials from them. HDPE in the form of heavy-duty industrial waste can be shredded into small particles, mixed with shredded empty drink cartons and compressed under heat to form a water-resistant building board. In these, the process uses the polyethylene content in the cartons (the waterproofing bit) to fuse and bond the materials together. Other manufacturers have employed extruded hollow-section technology to advantage by using purely recycled plastic to make garden decking boards, tongued-and-grooved boarding and other such products that have an inherent need for strength. The hollow construction creates a twin-wall design, improving its structural qualities by a considerable amount. This opens up the possibility of a range of products that might otherwise only be available from new material. Plastic bags can be recycled into plastic wood and building materials, but most supermarkets are favouring the decomposing, disposable-bag route. If you reuse them as liners in the kitchen pedal bin and have your waste taken away in them, they do virtually turn to dust within a year or so. At present plastic recycling centres won't take anything other than containers, and certainly styrofoam and PVC products are not wanted.

ALUMINIUM

Lightweight and strong, aluminium is a popular metal, being used for making drink cans the world over. So it is all the more important that we replenish the supply by recycling empties instead of burying them to corrode in landfill sites. What makes the idea of recycling cans even more attractive is the fact that currently it takes only six weeks to recycle a waste can back into a new one on the supermarket shelf. Furthermore the energy expended in doing this is only five per cent of that required to make new cans from raw materials. The world gets through a lot of aluminium cans, and recycling them makes a big difference to the environment. All that is necessary is for us to rinse them out in water and put them in the recycling bin for collection or take them to the local recycling centre.

GREEN WASTE

Plant waste from our gardens amounts to about 17 per cent and kitchen waste

MAKING YOUR OWN COMPOST

- Make sure your compost bin sits on bare soil, preferably in a sunny spot. You'll need the help of visiting worms, and they won't get through the concrete on the drive.

- Use kitchen waste, like vegetable peelings, eggshells, and even teabags and paper towels; all are beneficial. You can even empty the vacuum-cleaner bag into the bin.

- Mix the ingredients before you add them to the bin – kitchen waste with grass cuttings, twigs and leaves; layers of soft material and layers of chopped harder material.

- Be prepared to wait for up to a year before the compost is usable. When it has become dark, crumbly and moist with a fresh earthy smell in the bottom of the composter, the compost is ready. It pays to have two composters to ensure you always have a supply.

- Accelerate the process by retaining the heat, laying a piece of old carpet over the bin, and by adding fresh manure from stables and farms.

The recyclable aluminium and steel symbols

The recyclable plastic symbols

from rare peat reserves, special landscapes that should be protected. If the mass of green waste we produce could be composted, bagged and sold at a fair price, I can't help thinking that we would all benefit. Composting your own, of course, if you have the space, is an even better option.

Home composting isn't always successful, and I think it's partly because the mass of material isn't enough at any one time – community composting solves that. A high temperature of up to 60°C is needed in the centre, which requires a lot of organic material arriving in bulk. A European Union directive requires that 25 per cent of biodegradable waste is diverted away from landfill sites by 2010, and 65 per cent by 2050. Not only is it feasible for local authorities to collect garden waste and compost it, but also it is usually less costly than collecting it and disposing of it.

Composting isn't exactly a new science. Our ancestors were doing it hundreds of years ago; it's just that in more recent times, we have forgotten how beneficial it can be. Gardening is enjoying

14 per cent of all the waste we poduce, and most of it could be composted. Every year the gardeners of the world buy tonnes of bagged compost for planting and soil treatment, some of which is cut

something of a renaissance at the moment, with young homeowners taking it up much earlier than their parents did. Maybe it's a new aspect of consumerism that sees us buying plants and employing garden designers, rather than growing plants and creating gardens ourselves, but its gardening all the same, and you can't do without compost to improve the soil.

ENERGY USING PRODUCTS (EUPS)

These products deplete a fair proportion of natural resources and energy in their manufacture, regardless of whether they are electrical, or fossil-fuel or renewable-fuel powered. Consequently another directive has been established by the European Union to make producers more environmentally aware. That really applies to the design of products, because that is where 80 per cent of the damage is done, and where significant improvements can be made. There are lots of contradictions along the way with EuPs – washing machines, for example, run more economically at lower temperatures, but to clean clothes well at low temperatures, they need effective detergents, which pollute. Using less detergent means running the machine at a higher temperature and using more energy. Energy saving compact fluorescent lamps consume much less power than standard filament lamps, but to do so they must contain mercury, which is listed as a hazardous substance.

HAZARDOUS SUBSTANCES

You won't be surprised to know that the EU has a directive for these as well. The Restriction of Hazardous Substances directive bans some of the nasty metals

that have found their way into the ground and will stay there to contaminate it in the future. Metals that are harmful include lead, mercury, and cadmium. Chromium (VI), polybrominated biphenyls (PBBs) and polybrominated diphenyl ethers (PBDEs) are banned from July 2006.

There are exemptions for a few materials that are irreplaceable and found in low quantities, notably:

- The mercury used in lamps such as compact fluorescent light bulbs, where it is less than 5 mg.

- The lead used in the glass of cathode ray tubes and other electrical components.

- The lead used in alloying steel, copper and aluminium.

- The lead used in high-melting-point solders.

These materials are still banned from landfill sites and can't be included in your normal household waste. Mercury can be extracted from low-energy lamps and thermometers for reuse, so look for a facility or manufacturer who is doing this. Lead can be collected and re-employed if only in fishing weights.

REUSE

Renovating and repairing elements of your home, rather than replacing them, has become a little unfashionable, but now the emphasis is heading back towards restoration rather than replacement. For 25 years we've been ripping out perfectly sound timber windows and replacing them with PVC-u types; only now are we beginning to appreciate that timber windows are worth keeping because they have a dramatic effect on a home's character. Plastic windows have chunky, wide frames due to the inherent lack of strength in PVC-u, and that reduces the amount of glass, which in turn cuts down the light passing through them. They don't suit fanlights and small casements; sliding-sash types look awful; and fake glazing bars between the glass panes are the equivalent in poor taste of polystyrene ceiling tiles and embossed stone-effect cladding. I feel sure that one day in the not so distant future, owning badly designed and installed plastic windows will devalue a property, and we will be taking them out and replacing them with quality timber. That won't be a bad thing if we can find a way of recycling the plastic.

Casement windows are side hung and have been popular since the mid-18th century. They have the very good advantage of being easily maintained. Even if a timber casement has begun to rot, the hinges can be unscrewed and a new casement fitted. Likewise they are easy to reglaze, even with double-glazed units of considerable thickness.

Wooden sliding-sash windows are a little more demanding from a maintenance point of view, but they have a character that can't be replicated in any other material and are worth the effort for that reason alone. Boxes built into the sides of the frames conceal counterweights hung from cords that allow the window to stay open in any position. Often it is these counterweight systems that need attention to get the sashes rising and lowering smoothly again.

Invariably removing the layers of paint that have built up on them over the years helps too.

If you have wooden frames that are so rotten or impossible to reglaze, then replacing them is inevitable. Purpose-made timber windows are stronger and far more sustainable than plastic ones. Seek out a local joinery company; the result will be far more pleasing than the bulky frames of white plastic, particularly in a period property where the original windows were sliding sashes.

Adding shutters as protection for windows has been traditional in mainland Europe and North America for centuries. As well as helping to keep a house cool in summer, they also provide valuable security and protection from the wind. Shutters have traditionally been placed on the outside to accommodate inward opening windows, which is why they haven't been used in the UK.

Reusing something when it reaches the end of its life should be second nature, and for some of us this may be the case. In times of hardship, when products have been hard to come by or too expensive, finding substitutes for them in a 'make do and mend' approach to discarded items has been essential. Therein lies the problem today – we associate reuse with poverty and have convinced ourselves that second-hand is only for the poor, and that we should always buy new even if we have to borrow the money to do so.

That said, I think times are changing; second-hand products are becoming fashionable. Whether bought from car boot and garage sales or internet auction sites, second-hand items seem to be in demand. In fact finding a use for

145

something that otherwise would have been discarded is rewarding in itself – like cutting down and shaping a broken garden spade handle to form a dibber for planting bulbs; sometimes the products you make yourself aren't available in the shops. Not only does that make re-employing them rewarding, but also in some cases it can make them more valuable. I've met plenty of people who have salvaged stained glass and timber to make their own internal doors, which are unique to each room of their home and all the more valuable for it. Even if you don't have the skills to fashion joinery yourself, you can still salvage the materials and design the item for a specialist to make for you. Incidentally, even stained glass can be restored by an expert, and as with stonework restoration, finding someone can sometimes be done by contacting a local church or cathedral to find out who they've employed recently.

I've even seen cartwheels glazed and converted into circular windows. Often the only limit to what can be achieved through reuse is your imagination.

Architectural salvage is big business. It's an industry, valued at the turn of the 21st century at around one billion sterling a year in the UK alone. In our homes many of us have a passion for period features and quality craftsmanship that are hard to find in modern products. If something is available new, it comes at great expense, so finding salvaged materials and restoring them for reuse has become a popular trend. Actually reusing building materials isn't a new idea at all; it's been going on for centuries if not millennia. The remains from Roman buildings crop up in all kinds of places, as do stones from Egyptian and other ancient structures. It has always made sense to reuse what you could when building; it's only in recent years that we have tended to source all of our home-improvement materials from new. This is mainly because of speed, and the

Wooden window frames, unlike PVC-u, can be repaired

fact that sourcing and restoring old materials takes time, and time for new developers is the one thing they don't have. This has fuelled the market in architectural salvage from old buildings that are demolished or renovated.

Furniture, decorations, light fittings and garden features can all be reused. In gardens we can put almost anything to use as planters or wildlife nesting sites. We can also use all manner of objects to express our individual ideas in decorating our gardens. I've found that by shaping large roof slates and setting them in mortar, I can make a stepping-stone pathway and patio for my summerhouse that complements its slate roof visually and is damp-proof. Everything except the building's timber frame and cladding was a salvaged material. The building industry wastes huge amounts of unwanted material every day – years ago builders would store anything left over from jobs in their yards for use in the future, but now they tend to discard everything. Storage costs money, and selling something on is a hassle – and time is money to them. If you're stuck for architectural salvage in your area, check out local building sites and ask if you can look in the skips occasionally. Builders pay a lot to empty those skips, and most will be happy if you find something and remove it for them, so long as you don't endanger yourself in the process.

Ironwork

Ironwork was built to last. Any rust will usually be on the surface only and be easily cleaned off with fine steel wool and a rust remover. Methlylated spirit is good for cleaning, as opposed to water, which will only generate more rust. Red oxide and other rust inhibiting paints can then be used before normal primers and top coats, but painting isn't your only option. Outside you can simply clean up ironwork and give it a generous coating of linseed oil; indoors you can polish and buff it up with iron paste and a soft cloth. The latter is particularly effective on cast-iron fire surrounds. The condition of iron, as with timber, can be concealed with thick layers of paint, so it's important to buy salvage that has been stripped. That way you can be sure that is isn't falling apart at the seams.

Old wood

Reusing old timbers as beams is very satisfying, but remember that if it has been outside, timber will need to dry out thoroughly before being prepared and installed indoors.

Exposing the wood in floors and internal doors in older homes remains popular, but it can cause problems. In many cases internal doors are of a thin panel construction, with stiles and rails that aren't all that much thicker. Decades of over-painting will make them appear more substantial than they really are, and given the labour-intensive work of manually stripping them back to the bare wood, many of us simply deliver them to the acid bath. Having them dipped in sodium hydroxide accelerates the process, but not without costs. Firstly a door can take weeks to totally dry out afterwards, contaminating the air in your home as it does so. The process can also dissolve the glue in the joints and raise the grain in the timber to weaken the door and spoil its appearance. Lastly it can reveal just how badly made or damaged the door is.

Take your time, remove the door and stand it on a sheet outside before applying a brush-on paint stripper, leaving it overnight to soak in. The next day you'll be able to scrape off the old paint much more easily.

Sanitaryware

Antique bathroom sanitaryware remains popular, but the problem lies in restoring it to hygienic condition. There is very little that will do the task that isn't chemical-based. Products containing nasty stuff like ammonia and peroxide are applied by hand with cotton wool, followed by lime-scale removers, bleach and cream cleaning solutions. All in all, an arsenal of toxins that makes it essential to have antique sanitaryware renovated by specialists away from your home. I wouldn't recommend buying anything unless it was already restored – all that grime will do a fine job of concealing fine cracks that are common in porcelain and irreparable.

Provenance is the key word when buying architectural antiques. The market is riddled with stolen items, many sold for cash by unscrupulous dealers to unscrupulous buyers. Provenance is proof of authenticity as well as proof of previous ownership, forming a time line for any item. When buying make sure you get a receipt from the seller and some information about where they obtained it.

In truth about the only parts of a home that are not reuseable are the electrical wires and fittings, plus the plumbing pipes and equipment. Using old electrical hardware is a major health-and-safety risk, and legislation will stop you even if you're

daft enough to try. Plumbing pipes and the like have a hard life that leads to wear and failure; only when you can be sure the parts are relatively new and in good order should you buy them second-hand. Personally I would love to see a market for used heating equipment parts. As with cars, the manufacturers have succeeded in creating products that are short-lived and impossibly expensive to maintain so that we have to replace them frequently.

REDUCE

Reducing how much we consume doesn't just relate to energy; we consume products at a phenomenal rate, fed by an industry that aims to make them cheaper, and they are usually short-lived into the bargain. Our appetite for all things electronic is a prime example.

Electrical and electronic equipment

In the European Union about a million tonnes of electronic waste is produced per year, four per cent of the grand total, but it's growing at two or three times the rate of all other waste production. Some 75 per cent of the 'special' glass used by industry goes into these products, and over seven per cent of all the plastic used by Western Europeans is in there too. Nowhere are the three Rs more relevant in the 21st century than with electronic and electrical products. By and large they are cheap and evolve so quickly that they are soon outmoded. We always want to upgrade to the latest technology, which has meant disposing of the old model, even if it is in perfect working order, burying it in the ground. The UK manages to turn to waste six million items of electrical equipment every year, mainly TV sets, computers and mobile phones. This techno-lust sees us replacing our mobile phone every 18 months on average. In the USA 130 million phones are discarded to landfill per year with all their toxic ingredients (arsenic, antimony, beryllium, cadmium, copper, lead and nickel) intact. Most electrical gear contains nasty substances that aren't inert and therefore have a habit of leaking into the ground if taken to landfill. Lead, cadmium, mercury, hexavalent chromium, polybrominated biphenyls (PBBs) and polybrominated diphenyl ethers (PBDEs) have all been present, but will be phased out and eventually banned in many countries soon.

The WEEE (Waste from Electrical and Electronic Equipment) directive became law in Europe in 2005. It targets the manufacturers of these products and requires them to consider what happens to them at the end of their life, thus encouraging environmentally-friendly designs. It's a big U-turn for this industry, which to date seems to have been working towards equipment that is simply discarded when it goes wrong or becomes outmoded so that it can be replaced with the new and improved model. The WEEE directive will force manufacturers to be responsible for making their products more recyclable and for collecting end-of-life equipment.

Most equipment of this nature has its energy consumption firmly employed in the use phase of the product, but a few examples have a more overburdening manufacturing element, notably mobile phones. The extraction of metals and production of polymers from raw materials, together with the way these are

> ## COMPUTER POLLUTION
>
> It is believed that 250 million computers have been buried in landfill sites, adding not just 1.8 million tonnes of plastic, but also some rather sizeable quantities of undesirable metals – 450,000 tonnes of lead, 861 tonnes of cadmium, 544 tonnes of chromium and 181 tonnes of mercury. That vast amount of lead is in the cathode ray tubes of the monitors, where 2–3 kg can be found in each.
>
> Did you know that the flat-screen LCD laptops contain fewer toxins, but you can go even farther and buy biodegradable casings free of PVC, any nasty metals and PBDEs.

converted into products through the manufacturing process are problems. Not only that but their transportation to the consumer and end-of-life management are also evaluated to reveal a true statement of their environmental impact. All of that might be a bit pointless if a manufacturer doesn't recognize a product's environmental impact.

Thus it's important to link them with the relevant aspect of environmental harm – energy consumption = carbon emissions = climate change; acid emissions = acid rain = forest degradation; whether they affect the oxygen balance through eutrophication or damage the stratospheric ozone layer and so on. Where all this is meant to lead is to a clearer understanding, which with eco-labelling of all products, will indicate those products that are good and those that are not so good for the environment. We the consumers can then make informed choices about what we want to buy. At the moment we are a long way from a clear labelling scheme, and with different systems of labelling being adopted around the world, and the proliferation of global markets, consumer understanding seems a long way off. Hopefully that will change.

Reducing our use of non-renewable materials, like peat in the garden, is critical now. In doing so we can have an immediate effect on the environment. Marine aggregates are a good example.

Aggregates like sand, gravel and pebbles are widely used in construction and home improvement projects. Often they are quarried from inland sites, but not always. Dredging the seabed for them has been an essential way of meeting the high demand. Where it takes place, the industry is capable of removing millions of tonnes of sand and gravel every year from one licensed site alone.

Dredging is only carried out in shallow coastal waters, and it involves dragging anything between 2 and 4 m deep into the seabed, loading the material on to barges and bringing it ashore. The aggregate is sold on for use in preparing

sub-bases, concrete, patios, driveways, bedding for drainage pipes, and sand for bricklaying mortar and render.

As you might imagine, there is a limited quantity of aggregates that can be dredged, and the beds are essential breeding grounds for fish and marine invertebrates. A survey of the East English Channel gravel bank off the UK revealed it to be the home of over 150 different species. It is likely that the global reduction in fish stocks, has been aggravated by the removal of their gravel spawning grounds. Europe's North Sea has practically been dredged out, and like coal and oil, these aggregates are considered to be non-renewable, in this case having a permanent negative effect on marine diversity.

If these reasons aren't enough for you to steer clear of marine aggregates, you might also consider the effect their dredging has on the protection of our shoreline. The sea defences of our coastlines don't stop with the walls and beach groynes built by man, but largely with the aggregate banks that lie offshore. If these natural barriers are removed, the result will be a rise in coastal flooding and shore erosion, as have already been seen in areas that have been dredged.

Even washed marine aggregates can be identified by the presence of shells like scallops. So before you order, check the origin of the material and ask your supplier for quarried aggregate or recycled aggregate instead. Recycled products like colliery shale, concrete fines (waste from ready-mix plants) and road scrapings can be used as alternatives in some situations.

DANGERS OF MARINE AGGREGATES

Problems with marine aggregates can be caused because the salt content reacts with cement, so it has to be washed before the aggregate can be used. In countries where cheap materials are sought, it is common to find the beaches being dredged for sand. Without washing this thoroughly to remove its salt, structures are weakened considerably – concrete is attacked by sulphates, and masonry crumbles. The Turkish earthquake (August 1999) saw many buildings collapse disastrously because of this.

CHAPTER SEVEN

Water

Sea levels may rise with climate change, but the fresh water in our lakes and reservoirs is dropping. A combination of reduced rainfall, higher evaporation and increased demand from an expanding population makes water a precious resource. In North America, home of the Great Lakes, the water level of the largest five has been dropping annually – a significant marker because Lakes Superior, Huron, Michigan, Erie and Ontario represent between them a fifth of the world's surface fresh water, covering 518,000 sq.km. Of course water levels have always gone up and down, but in recent years they have dropped much more quickly than in the past. Lake Huron in Canada has seen a drop of more than 1 m in the Georgian Bay region.

Clean, drinkable water brings us life and good health, but we waste far more than we use. Not all of the world is stressed for water, but those areas where population demand almost outweighs supply include Pakistan, northern China, Morocco, south-east England, eastern Spain, Somalia, eastern Bulgaria and south-east Italy to name but a few. A great many other regions could be following close behind, from India to California, where 90 per cent of the wetlands have disappeared. The list is growing and likely to continue to do so as our demand for water increases. The average American uses about 455 litres of water per day, compared to around 32 litres per day used by the inhabitants of other less profligate nations. Water comes not just with wealth, but also with availability of source. Las Vegas, a desert town, has expanded rapidly since the building of the

Hoover Dam at Lake Powell, which ensures a good supply. Ironically the residents of the city use water at double the national rate, much of it for watering their lawns and gardens in the heat.

But reservoirs can only hold so much. In many areas they rely on the average winter rainfall to meet demand through the summer. When the winter rain doesn't fall, and the levels in spring are well below average, hosepipe bans are soon issued, followed by water rationing if things get really bad. You might think the answer lies with the sea, particularly if sea levels are on the up, but desalination of sea water is an option that only the super rich can afford. The wealthier desert countries of the Persian Gulf, like Dubai, have been able to use this process to meet most of their fresh-water needs. Because much less than one per cent of the Earth's water is usable to us, we need to conserve as much as we can. Water demand in our homes has risen from around 500 cu.km to 5,000 cu.km globally over the last century; we now use 45 times as much water as we did three centuries ago.

Conserving water

Water is a difficult substance to transport. When we do move it through buried pipes, we tend to lose large quantities through undetected leaks. Conserving water in water-rich regions does nothing to help those in water stressed regions if the surplus can't be transported to them. In most cases it can't, so if water conservation is to work at all, it has to be on a local level. You can't get more localized than household conservation measures. You may never be able to become self-sufficient for water (unless you can sink your own borehole to an aquifer), but reducing the amount of water you consume is the first step, and it is surprisingly easy to do.

Taking showers instead of baths, reducing the capacity of WC cisterns, only using the washing machine for full loads, reducing the amount used in your garden are all measures that can help. If you dedicate yourself to all four, you could reduce your water demand by as much as 50 per cent. Having your water metered is the only way to measure your success, and most supply companies will provide the equipment, often for free in stressed regions. With your level of demand under control, the next step could be to meet some of your needs through recycling and rainwater harvesting. In fact recycling is carried out by most water companies in developed countries, by diverting waste water to treatment plants, where it is cleansed before being reintroduced to the mains supply. It's an expensive process that only affects a third of the world's waste water at present. Even where it is done efficiently, however, recycling usually only tops up the supply. In the US city of St Petersburg, Florida, for example, which prides itself on water conservation, only a fifth of its supply comes from recycling; the rest has to be drawn from natural sources. What makes a difference is when individuals recycle for themselves and combine this with reduced consumption, but how easy is this to achieve?

RECYCLING WASTE WATER

Waste water can be divided into two categories – 'grey' and 'black'. 'Grey' waste water comes out of our homes having been used for washing and cooking; 'black' comes out of our homes through the waste pipes of the toilets. The former is carried by the waste pipes from sinks, basins, showers, baths, washing machines and dishwashers to join with the rest. Recycling 'black' water, or sewage, isn't something that most of us would want to get into, even if it was achievable, but you'll find information on compost toilets for the garden on the internet. Where recycling is concerned, we are dealing exclusively with 'grey' water. Much of this is practically clean to begin with, since it may only have been used for rinsing your hands or sloshing around the basin. Some will be heavily polluted with detergents or salt, however, where it has been pumped out of the washing machine or dishwasher. The point is that although we can clean it up a bit, we can't clean it sufficiently to be potable – suitable for cooking or drinking. Such water can be re-employed in toilet cisterns. In a family home a toilet cistern of 6 litres might be flushed a dozen times a day, washing away 72 litres of drinkable water. Imagine buying 72 bottles of mineral water every day and pouring it down the toilet. It will soon focus your mind on what you could achieve by installing a recycling system.

To begin with what you need is a storage tank of some description, one that is sized to meet your needs plus some spare capacity. The tank must have an overflow that carries away surplus water to the drains, which is where it was heading in the first place, so think of the tank as a stop along the way where it can be re-employed. Waste water from the kitchen sink, hand basins, shower and bath could all be diverted to this tank, from where it can be piped to the toilet cisterns in your home. Of course the mains water supply arrives under considerable pressure, which means that you can plumb in a toilet cistern several floors up without having to pump the water to it, but a pump will be needed for recycled water. If the storage tank is underground beneath the garden, you will need to pump the water from it to a second storage tank in the loft. From here the supply to the toilets can operate under gravity on demand, no adaptation of the standard cistern's plumbing being necessary. A cistern may take a little longer to refill after flushing when fed by a gravity supply compared to mains pressure, but that will be the only difference. The alternative would be to pump the waste water directly to a header tank for reuse.

Even 'grey' water used in toilets should be cleaned up in the interests of hygiene. Simple filtration should be enough, but more advanced screening with UV (ultra-violet) light is possible. That however is taking us into the realms of water polishing, the purpose of which is to reduce bacteria in the water. There are waste water pumps that can be installed to raise macerated water from sinks and dishwashers to a high-level header tank, and if you choose this method, you could employ one to serve several kitchen appliances (sink, washing machine, dishwasher, etc). In truth macerators have been designed and marketed not to recycle waste water, but to allow appliances to be installed where they are below a gravity-fed drainage system – the basement conversion market. They work

automatically as water arrives in the system to liquidize any semi-solids with the water and pump them on, usually via a 25 mm diameter pipe. In this case, instead of pumping it to the drainage system, it could pump it to a header tank in the roof space. The tank would need to be adequately sized (around 400 litres) and fitted with overflow pipes to the mains drainage to cope with the flow rate of the water arriving. In the absence of effective filtration and some purification of 'grey' water, it can't be used without causing problems. In the garden the soluble detergents and salts in it will kill off your plants and probably clog up any irrigation pipes quite quickly.

In fact toilet cisterns are the only viable users of recycled 'grey' water, and you should be able to keep them filled with water from hand basins, baths and showers alone. When a plumbing system is installed to collect the waste from appliances used for human washing, you can improve the water quality by using less-aggressive detergents for cleaning them.

If you don't fancy pumping the waste water directly to a header tank, an external storage tank could be installed to serve a gravity-fed waste system. Since the appliances concerned are usually connected by separate and smaller waste pipes to the main ('black' water) soil pipes, some plumbing alterations will be required. It is likely that a separate 75 mm grey soil stack will need to serve this system and carry the waste to the storage tank. Fine-gauze filters would need to be incorporated, and these would need to be removed and cleaned frequently. Recycling waste water is not problem-free, and because of this you may find greater advantage in harvesting rainwater.

RAINWATER HARVESTING

In the past rainwater cisterns were a common feature of homes. Brick built and lined with render, they were installed close to, if not inside, the kitchen or laundry room, water being drawn in by hand pump for washing. I have lost count of the number of these cisterns I have seen that had been discovered when people were extending their homes, but as yet I haven't met one person who wanted to re-employ one. Rainwater always seems to be a problem today – either we have too much of it or too little. Too much results in flooding and ground saturation, so the whole concept of rainwater drainage is about disposal –

getting rainwater off roofs and pavements and away from our buildings. After periods of heavy rain, it isn't just the swollen rivers that threaten us: drains swamped with storm water can back up, causing manhole covers to lift under the pressure and water to surge right back to our pavements and backyards. Flooding may be a threat every year, but often so is drought, when a lack of rain forces us to conserve water. Instead of wondering why it is that we spend so much trying to get water away from our homes, and then so much trying to get it back again, we could change our thinking and harvest rainwater as if it were a crop. Up to two-thirds of the non-potable water used in the average home could be recycled rainwater. The water-use pie-chart on page 156 shows how our water needs

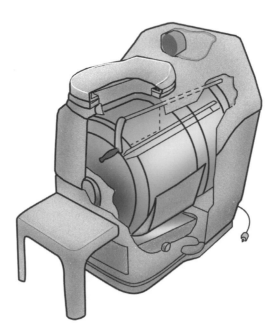

Composter toilet

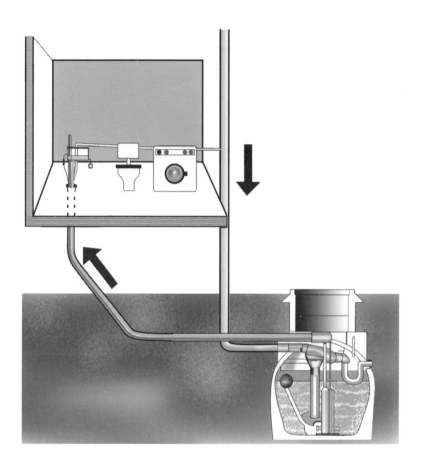

Rainwater recycling system

are divided. You can see that a quarter of it is flushed straight down the pan.

BENEFITS OF RAINWATER HARVESTING

● It reduces your demand for mains water and (if your supply is metered) the cost.

● It reduces the risk of flooding from overburdened drains and waterlogged ground.

● It reduces the problems caused by hard water, such as limescale, to your washing machine and WC plumbing.

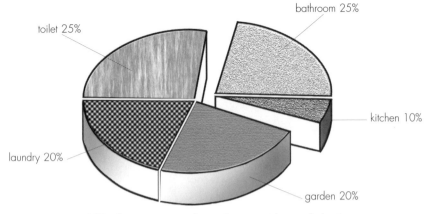

toilet 25%

bathroom 25%

kitchen 10%

laundry 20%

garden 20%

Up to 65% of our water needs can be met with recycled rainwater

• It allows you to irrigate your garden long after hosepipe bans have been enforced in times of drought (when your plants need water the most).

• It is essential for some plants (eg. lime-hating species such as azaleas, camellias and hydrangeas) to receive soft rainwater and not hard, chemically treated mains water that can cause chlorosis.

• It is good for topping up ponds in the summer when evaporation rates are high, putting fish and wildlife at risk.

HOW MUCH RAIN CAN I COLLECT?

Rain from your roof is easily collected, and given most roof coverings it is much cleaner than run-off from the ground. Storm water from a patio or pathway could be collected, but any water running off of driveways should be avoided, since it may be polluted with oil and fuel from your car. For your home the roof is the primary collector. Calculating its surface area and multiplying this by the annual rainfall for your location will give you a volume of water per annum. Because 1 cu.m equates to 1000 litres, it is easy to establish how many litres a day you can expect to collect. You can't avoid some loss though, through spillage and evaporation, and your calculations should allow a drop of 10–20 per cent in this respect.

Here is an example of the calculation: roof area of 12 m x 5 m = 60 sq.m x average annual rainfall of 0.60 m = 36 cu.m x 1000 = 36,000 litres less ten per cent = 32,400 litres collected.

HOW MUCH RAINWATER DO I NEED TO STORE?

This requires a similar calculation, but one based on demand rather than supply. How much you use is estimated per person in the household. It needs to be based on the worst case, because you are estimating your storage needs during an assumed drought. If you're supplying the washing machine, WC's and garden in the summer, that could amount to 50 litres per person per day.

Rainwater harvesting systems

FOUR ESSENTIAL FEATURES COMMON TO ALL RAINWATER HARVESTING SYSTEMS

1 Filtration of the water running off roofs and paving is essential before it is stored.

2 Storage is in tanks, usually below ground.

3 Pumping of the stored water back to a header tank that supplies the appliances using it, or direct to the point of use.

4 Overflow protection to release surplus water to disposal.

Use this formula to determine annual usage: C x n x 365 = L (where C is consumption in litres per person per day; n is number of people in household; L is litres required per annum).

Use this formula to determine the amount of stored water required during a dry period: (L x t) ÷ 365 = litres of storage needed (where L is litres required per annum; t is time in days of average longest dry period).

For example: 50 x 4 x 365 = 73,000 litres of storage (50 litres per day per person for four people); (73,000 x 30) ÷365 = 6000 litres tank size (assuming a 30-day drought period).

THE PROCESS AND COMPONENTS OF RAINWATER HARVESTING

The following are the basic elements of rainwater harvesting, but the construction of the system depends very much on what you do with the water.

Collecting the rain

The rainwater harvesting route begins on the roof of your home. Most roof coverings do not present a problem to rainwater collection. The greatest risk of contamination is likely to come from lead flashings and gutters; in some countries, like the UK, valley gutters are traditionally lined with lead. Rainwater, given its slightly acidic ph value, can dissolve small amounts of lead, which pollute the water. This is not suitable for consumption and shouldn't be introduced to the food chain by using it to water a vegetable garden. Other roof materials, such as asbestos tiles and asphalt, can also contaminate water and will restrict the use to which you can put it. If there is a risk of contamination, avoid using the water for washing and certainly irrigating a vegetable garden. Used in toilet cisterns, it shouldn't present a problem.

Unless the rainwater gutters and pipes of your home are asbestos, they will be suitable for continued use, as long as they are adequately sized and cleaned out periodically. Asbestos gutters should be removed by a specialist contractor who is licensed to dispose of them safely. In most cases either PVC-u or aluminium gutters and pipes will be fitted, and the pipework carrying the water to the storage tank can be continued in PVC-u. If it is to be run below ground, then pipework of at least 100 mm diameter manufactured for buried drainage should be used. Lay it in a trench on a bed of pea shingle or gravel to a gradient (fall) of about 1:40. Do not be tempted to lay rainwater downpipes below ground; they are neither large enough nor strong enough to be used in this way and will soon deform or crack.

Primary filtration and screening

Proprietary fittings are available to prevent leaves and debris from entering the storage tank. Essentially they are stainless steel mesh screens with a gauge of between 3 and 6 mm. They will need regular cleaning to prevent them from blocking the flow, so it is important that they are accessible. Gutter mesh can be fitted along the whole length of the gutter if you are prepared to get up there and clean it off regularly. A rainwater hopper head fitted with a screen might be less of a problem to maintain, or you might prefer to form a trap and filter at the entrance to the tank itself. The latter appeals to me, simply because it would be so much easier to clean out. A small interceptor or gully could be used to collect the unwanted debris, with a mesh screen added to its outlet. I've not actually seen this arrangement described anywhere, so you may have to make your own from standard drainage fittings, but that shouldn't prove difficult.

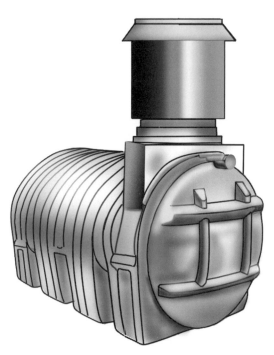

Propriety rainwater storage tank

STORAGE TANK CAPABILITIES						
Purpose	Water use (litres)	Tank capacity (litres)				
		200*	1000	3000	4500	9000
WC only	125	50%	80%	95%	100%	100%
WC and washing machine	225	40%	65%	85%	90%	100%
WC, washing machine and garden use	325	35%	50%	70%	80%	90%
* Water butt						

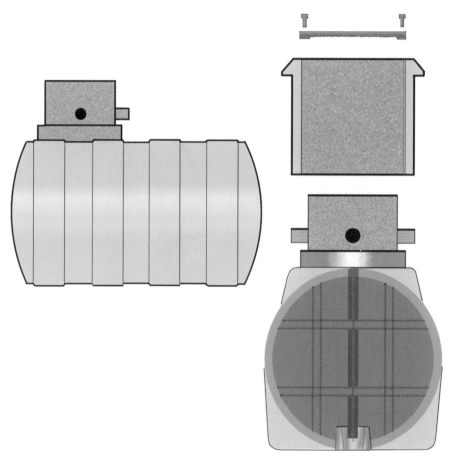

Sizing rainwater storage tanks

Proprietary first-flush diverters

These devices are intended to automatically divert the first flush of rainwater into the normal disposal system, whether it be a soakaway or drainage system. In this way most of the debris washed off the roof when it starts to rain is prevented from entering the storage tank. About the first 40 litres of water for every 100 sq.m of roof is diverted into a small chamber (like an interceptor or gulley), and once this is filled the remainder enters the tank. The chamber often has a small hole with a pipe in the bottom that allows the first flush to drain away slowly afterwards.

Storage tanks

Having got the water from the roof and through an initial screening process, we now have to store it. Look into any water butt and you'll see all manner of life, from mosquito larvae to tadpoles, wiggling about. Water attracts wildlife. If you are going to store rainwater, it must be sealed against insects, rodents, birds and small children. It also needs to be kept in the dark if algae aren't to grow. An underground sealed tank is the only sensible solution. Fibreglass (GRP) tanks are manufactured for this purpose, as indeed they are for foul water as cesspools. In cesspool form, a capsule-

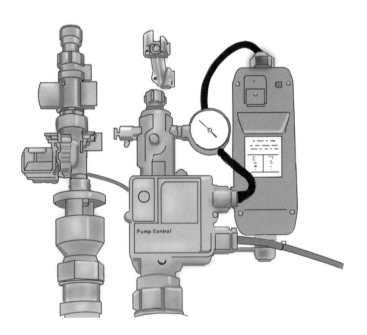

Water management controls of a rainwater harvesting system

shaped tank will have a single opening on top with an extended neck shaft. This neck will contain an inlet for the water, but also a vent pipe outlet because foul water contains methane gas. Using a cesspool for rainwater storage means sealing up this outlet or connecting it to an overflow. Since they start at 18 cu.m (18,000 litres) capacity, however, a cesspool is likely to be too large for your needs. Furthermore GRP cesspools are very expensive compared to septic tanks. These bulb-shaped vessels are also adaptable for rainwater harvesting, and you may be able to find a smaller size that suits. Remember: the bigger the tank, the bigger the hole that must be dug for it. In heavy waterlogged soils, like clay, these tanks have a habit of popping out of the ground like corks. Consequently it is

essential that the holes are backfilled with concrete to prevent this.

Specialist companies manufacture rainwater tanks complete with overflows and submersible pumps that are activated by float switches. These tanks are available in a variety of sizes starting at 1000 litres and ranging up to 9000 litres. Even at 4500 litres, a medium-sized model will cut the peak rainwater flow into the sewers by a third, reducing the risk of flooding due to overburdened drains. The table on page 159 shows the average annual percentage of water supplied by the various tank sizes. The figures are based on a roof area of 150 sq.m. A 200 litre tank (water-butt size) is also included as a point of reference, but being so small, this would only be able to supply half the water needed for toilet flushing.

Linked rainwater butts via overflows

Pumps and supply

The system won't work at all if the pump isn't capable of lifting the water from the tank to the point of use. All pumps have a maximum height for raising water, which will need checking. They should also be fitted with fine-gauze filters to ensure that they aren't damaged or clogged by dirt. Even with all these precautions, the water may still have collected airborne bacteria, or become contaminated by bird or rodent droppings; only by screening with UV light or chemicals can this bacteria be eliminated. I don't think this is necessary, but as the last line of defence, an in-line cartridge filter should be plumbed into the appliance supply pipe. These are simple washable 80 micron filters, which are commonly used for swimming pools.

Break tanks

An internal break tank is often supplied to feed existing appliances by gravity. For this all that is needed is a conventional water tank located in the roof space, with a float valve and overflow system to guard against over-filling. Like any cold-water tank, it should have a sealed lid and be insulated against the risk of freezing in a cold roof space.

Integrated systems

Because rainwater can't be guaranteed, you will need a mains water supply as a back-up to any appliance, but most importantly to toilet cisterns. The integrated system should use rainwater as the primary source, and only when the supply is exhausted should it open the mains supply. An integrated system like this runs the risk of contaminating the potable mains water, so water regulations

Garden water collection butt

will require that backflow-prevention measures (such as double check valves) are included in the plumbing to protect it.

Monitoring the system

Regularly checking the water quality and staying alert to changes in its colour and smell is advisable, even though you will not be using it for potable purposes. You should also inspect and maintain the system, keeping the gutters clean and free-flowing, and tank lids secure. For the gadget-minded there are microprocessor management systems that display the volume of water in storage, switch pumps off when it drops too low and switch to mains water when needed.

CONSERVING WATER IN THE GARDEN

You can do a lot before summer to reduce the volume of water needed in your garden to maintain plants. Adding organic material and mulch to the soil before planting helps a good deal. Banking up the soil slightly at the bases of shrubs to form a 'moat' aids watering by keeping it where it's needed. When you do water, do so thoroughly – apply a whole watering can full to established shrubs, filling the moat. Watering infrequently in this way is far better than giving small amounts of water frequently, which will encourage poor root development and spindly growth. Watering cans are good for dealing with small and individual plants, but in some cases you can end up using more water than you would with a hose. I've found that a hose with a trigger gun fitting, which will direct a jet of water exactly where needed, offers the most conservative water use.

Low-water gardening

As the demands on our water supply increase, it makes sense to reduce the amount of water needed in gardening first. In times of drought, hosepipe bans are inevitable, so if you can create a low-water-demand garden, even if your rainwater store runs dry, it won't suffer.

Water has a price wherever you live, and in most temperate zones we can't direct too much into our gardens. Sprinklers have no purpose at all anymore; I'm not sure that they ever did, but allowing one to spray water around an established lawn is bordering on criminal. Grass is a hardy species that survives drought. True it goes brown and its growth slows, but it also greens up when the rain returns. Wherever the annual rainfall is below 450 mm, lawns will be brown for some of the year. When we garden now, we tend to construct an outdoor living space with hard surfacing and structural features as well as plants; for these 'garden rooms', it is easy to find low-water-demand plants.

TREATING THE RAINWATER

- Rainwater used for garden purposes requires little, if any, filtration, although you do need to take some steps to ensure that irrigation systems and hose nozzles don't become clogged if you plan on pumping water directly from the store to the plants.

- Rainwater used in a toilet cistern for flushing requires a little more treatment, since the water may be held in the cistern for some time before being discharged, while the pan needs to be cleaned by the flushing water and not contaminated by it. You can do this in a number of ways, but first it's important that the water held in the primary storage tank outside is not exposed to light that would promote algae growth. Buried tanks eliminate this risk. The water can also be chlorinated annually in the tank to reduce contamination; at the very least a disinfectant block can be inserted in the toilet cistern.

- Rainwater for laundry and toilet cisterns requires very fine filtration and cleaning, although in some countries neither is required for water that is non-potable. There are additives that can be released into the storage tank to help settle the sediments or balance the pH reading.

Soil type

The soil and its ability to retain moisture have a large part to play in determing the species that will survive. Peat and clay will dry out at times, but hold moisture for much longer than sandy and gravel soils. I live in an area of clay soil that becomes desiccated every year in summer, but it is deceptive – on the surface it has all the hardness of concrete with cracks large enough to lose a cat in, but a metre below the moisture is still there. When trenches are dug in clay, you get a clear view of the transition from the dry, fractured material near the surface into the moist cohesive soil deeper down. The zone of desiccation is deepened considerably by trees as their roots search for water. Generally, however, the subsoil never seems to dry out completely, and many deep-rooted plants will survive in clay soils, but not in others. Plants that do suffer are the shallow-rooted types, so you'll need to grow these in containers if you still want them.

For sandy or gravel soils, which are better drained, flowering shallow-rooted species that require no additional watering once established are not hard to find. Kniphofia, achillea and lychnis, plus a wide variety of colourful poppies from California and the Mediterranean, are all excellent in hot, dry gardens.

Trees are a bit of a double-edged sword: they can have a cooling effect on a garden during hot weather by providing a canopy of dense leaves to block out the sun's radiation. Walk into a deciduous wood on a hot day, and the temperature drops to a welcoming coolness that you won't find anywhere else. On the other hand, trees need water – lots of it.

Soil improvement

You can help the ground to retain water by mulching around plants to keep the soil cool and reduce evaporation. Cocoa shells are great for this, although the smell of chocolate doesn't last as long as I'd like and eventually a web of white fungus starts to spread over it. Forest bark is usually the shredded droppings of pine trees and also does the job well, but keep it away from plant stems because it will

stop them from getting any water at all in the summer; in winter it can become saturated for months, causing them to rot.

I've heard of soil conditioning, but this always seems to involve double digging or something equally robust; instead I've discovered that covering the heavy clay in my garden with a layer of imported topsoil is far easier. The new material is less than 300 mm thick, but it provides a perfect growing medium for everything that is shallow-rooted and keeps the clay below moist for everything deep-rooted. You can add composted material, sharp sand and grit to improve the drainage of clay if it gets really boggy in winter – this is a condition that will kill off plants far more efficiently than anything else.

filter

hose connection

central unit reduces water pressure

connector for

drip heads

spike

cleaning tool

Components of an irrigating drip system

Watering efficiently

How we water our plants makes a lot of difference to the amount of water used and to the plants' growth. Frequently applying small amounts of water will lead to shallow surface roots and weak plants; an occasional decent deluge applied directly to the base of the plant is far better. Pushing in a watering pipe next to the plant when you plant it will provide a channel that ensures the water gets to where it matters, the roots.

Special hoses that allow water to seep through fine holes along their length are excellent if you bury them beneath a layer of mulch, but you will need to prevent the soil or mulch from blocking the holes, and the best way of doing this is to lay them in shallow beds of shingle or grit. In doing so you create a miniature irrigation trench that will leach water around the plants' roots. Some seep hoses are made from the rubber of recycled car tyres, and I can't think of a better use for it.

Even drought-resistant plants will need watering when they are first introduced, but given some protective mulching and water applied directly beneath them, they will reach a stage when they will continue to grow with very little watering. If you grow your own vegetables, give up on the runner beans – they need a lot of watering – concentrate instead on root crops, like onions, potatoes and carrots.

Annuals, I'm afraid, are too much effort for me. They require such a lot of nurturing and protection from slugs and snails, not to mention frost protection and watering, just to get them established that I've decided they aren't worth the effort any more. The gardening world has so much more to offer in perennials and shrubs, so many of which are drought tolerant.

LOW-WATER-DEMAND PERENNIALS

Achillea	Helichrysum
Agapanthus (African Lily)	Iris
Agave	Kniphofia (Red-hot Poker)
Allium	Lavandula (Lavender)
Asclepias (Butterfly Weed)	Lychnis
Brachyscome (Swan River Daisy)	Nepeta (Catmint)
Calendula (Pot Marigold)	Oenothera (Evening Primrose)
Cosmos	Papaver (Poppy)
Dictamnus (Burning Bush)	Phormium (New Zealand Flax)
Echinops (Globe Thistle)	Potulaca
Eryngium (Sea Holly)	Salvia
Erysimum (Wallflower)	Sedum
Eschscholzia (California Poppy)	Tulipa (Tulip)
Euphorbia (Barrenwort)	Verbascum
Gazania	Verbena

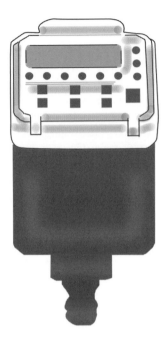

Water programmer for a drip irrigation system

LOW-WATER-DEMAND CLIMBING PLANTS AND SHRUBS

Bougainvillea

Buxus (Box)

Caragana (Pea Tree)

Cordyline (Cabbage Palm)

Cotoneaster

Cytisus (Broom)

Euonymus

Hebe

Hedera (Ivy)

Lavatera

Lonicera (Honeysuckle)

Nerium

Palms

Spartium (Spanish Broom)

Yucca

Harvesting and managing water are key elements in a successful eco-home conversion, but once you have carried them out – as with all the projects in this book – you will have reduced your home's impact on its environment and improved the environment around your home. Your eco-friendly home will have a sense of serenity and harmony built into its very fabric, making it a joy to return to, and giving you a sense of belonging that will make it hard to leave.

Epilogue

It's time to settle the climate-change bill

In the words of the legendary American baseball player, Lawrence Peter (Yogi) Berra,

'The future ain't what it used to be.'

It seems we have all been rather indulgent with the world's resources, at least in the developed world. Flicking a switch on for power whenever we want it, forgetting to flick it off when we don't; burning gas and oil for heat and letting it flow through our homes and out; letting the tap run, so to speak, on every aspect of our lives. And very nice it's been too. But like every credit card shopper, we kind of knew that there would be a price to pay for our excesses, but that was in the future. Now it seems that the bill has arrived, and we are all being encouraged to peek inside the envelope to see how much we've spent. Those of us who have already looked may still be in shock; others might have moved on to denial. Which means, of course, that the next step is to try to come up with a payment plan, I say plan because it seems the bill is unthinkably large and impossible to pay off in one go. In fact we are going to have to pass on some of the debt to our children and indeed to their children.

As this is being written environmental science is still very new to us. Our accuracy in forecasting tomorrow's weather has got better, but stretch the forecast to next week and it often falls apart. Predicting the future's weather is clearly beyond us, and trying to establish by how much the planet is warming or cooling, or whether it is staying the same, is hopelessly beyond us. Where I live the weather often changes from year to year. I say that not because of what I've read, but because I have been keeping my own daily weather diary since 1975. In the last 30 years we have had hot summers, cold summers, dry summers and wet summers; ditto for the other seasons. The only pattern that I've seen in that time is that the cold weather we expect in winter tends to arrive later now, often in January. Having said that, my home town has expanded greatly in the last decade and become enveloped by a mile-deep ring of housing, and an urban environment is usually warmer than a rural one. We are constantly being told, however, that global warming is real, the argument having been settled not with predictions, but with measurements – it has started to happen. The predictions were threatening enough and most of us were happier to stick our heads in the sand and not think about them; now it seems that those predictions could have been wildly miscalculated. Apparently the scientific community hadn't realized that the effects had been reduced by our own pollution. During the 20th century we released a good deal of pollution into the atmosphere and, not surprisingly, it reduced sunlight levels around the globe, by an average of ten per cent. Over the last decade, however, we have cleaned up the air significantly. This fact hadn't been appreciated, let alone built into the climate-prediction programs. Now that we are cleaning up our air quality, at least in Europe, sunlight levels are returning to normal and we will no longer be shielded from the temperature rise – the full effect of our carbon filled atmosphere is making itself felt, and the corrected predictions are inescapably dire, even from beneath the sand.

Even if climate change is natural, if only in part, it doesn't matter, because we also contribute to it in an overly generous manner. What matters is that we slow it down and reduce its effects as quickly as we can. Individually of course we know it to be hopeless, but collectively it most certainly isn't. Collectively we have sent, and continue to send about 2 billion tonnes of carbon dioxide into the atmosphere every year; collectively, if we choose, we could send much, much less. If you've ever been amazed at how many people vote in TV talent shows or how much money we can raise for a charity in a few short weeks after a disaster, you'll understand that the power we have is in our number, as a population. In a population individuals only have to make small changes to yield big consequences.

So you could consider this book a means of starting to settle the climate-change bill. Some of the ideas in it will seem too minor to have any consequence, and individually they are, but collectively they will make a difference.

Glossary

Attenuation
Evening out the flow of water over a long time period to reduce the flow at peak times.

Balancing pond
A garden pond that stores rainwater run-off to reduce the flow to a drain or soakaway.

Biomass Fuel
Fuel oil derived from decomposed plant and vegetable matter.

Breathable construction
A vapour permeable construction that allows moisture to pass through it, rather than condense on it.

Candela
The SI unit of luminous intensity. You could consider it to be a measure of the brightness of a lamp.

Carbon emission rating
By making energy efficiencies in the home, you should not only reduce the cost of living in it, but also reduce its carbon emission rate. This rate is measured as the mass of carbon (CO_2) in kilograms (kg) per total floor area in square metres per year.

Cellulose insulation
The generic name for pulped recycled paper insulation materials.

CFC
Chlorofluorocarbons are used in aerosols, fridges and also solvents, and contribute to the depletion of the ozone layer.

Combi boiler
Combination boilers heat water on demand in pressure systems without the need for storage tanks.

Condensing boiler
High energy efficiency boilers that run at lower temperatures with built-in heat exchangers to cool and condense the exhaust gases.

Daylight shelf
Devices fitted at the top part of window openings, directly below ceiling level, to reflect light further into the room.

Eco-design
The integration of environmental issues in the design of products with the object of improving environmental performance throughout their life cycle.

Ecological profile
A description of something that has been measured in terms of inputs, outputs, raw materials, emissions and wastes throughout its life cycle from the point of view of its environmental impact.

EMF
Electro-magnetic fields generate radiation and consist of both electrical and magnetic waves at right angles to each other and the source. They are propagated by all electrical devices.

End of life
The end of a product's first use.

Gabions
Cages of wire-mesh loose filled with rocks often used to act as retaining walls but also as natural heat stores.

Grey water
Waste water from sinks, baths, showers and appliances. Water from kitchen sinks and dishwashers is not normally collected for reuse because of the fats, detergents and salts that it contains.

GWP
Global Warming Potential – a measurement of a materials capacity to cause global warming, through it's whole life cycle from extraction and manufacture to use. It compares the warming caused by a similar mass of carbon dioxide. Replacing ODP in many countries.

HFC
Hydro-fluorocarbons are commonly found in household products such paints and detergents but also in synthetic fibres and perfumes.

Joule
The unit with which energy consumption is measured.

K value
The thermal conductivity of a material.

Kilowatt-hour
The quantity of power used by an appliance.

Life cycle
The period of a product's life, from design to final disposal.

Lumens
Also describes as flux, lumens can be thought of as the strength of light emitted or reflected.

Lux
The illumination on a surface (from one lumen per square metre).

ODP
Ozone Depletion Potential – a measurement of a materials capacity to create 'greenhouse gases' likely to deplete the ozone layer. Look for zero ODP in eco-friendly materials.

Payback Time
A measurement of economic value, calculated to establish how long it will take the savings gained by a conversion project to pay for the cost of that project. Once payback time has elapsed, the project starts to save you money.

PBDE
Polybrominated diphenyl is used as a flame retarding substance in many products, such as carpets and furnishings, but it is readily absorbed into the environment and our bodies.

PIR
Passive Infra-Red – technology employed in detectors for automatic switching of lights, extractor fans, security alarms, etc.

PV

Photo-voltaic solar panels that convert UV light into electricity.

R value

The thermal resistance of a material or an element (e.g. wall or roof).

Recycling

Reprocessing waste materials to reproduce the same product, or make a new product, excluding energy extraction.

Run-off

Rainwater flowing off roofs and the ground into the drainage system.

Soakaway

An underground storage structure that collects rainwater and allows it to filter into the subsoil away from buildings.

Solar gain

The internal heat generated by the sun through thermal transmission.

Solar irradiation

Exposure to sunlight (predicted by orientation, angle and shading).

TRV

Thermostatic Radiator Valve – a manual control valve fitted to each radiator that can be used to control the flow of hot water into it and prevent it from overheating the room or heating it when the room is not in use.

U Value

The rate of heat transmission through an element (e.g. wall or roof).

VOC

Volatile Organic Compounds are able to change from liquid or solid form to a vapour that can be inhaled, to the potential detriment of health. They are present in many materials, furnishings, paints and adhesives.

Waste

Any object or substance that is discarded, or required or intended to be discarded.

Watts

The power output on an appliance, measured as a rate.

WEEE

Waste from electrical and electronic equipment is the waste of the modern age, with discarded computers, TV's and mobile cell phones increasing rapidly.

W/m.sq.deg.k

The rate of heat loss through an element (e.g. wall or roof).

Useful Contacts

Association of Environment Conscious Building (AECB)
PO Box 32,
Llandysul SA44 5ZA
Tel 0845 456 9773
www.aecb.net

BRE Ltd
Garston
Watford WD25 9XX
Tel: 08702 430 930
(Scotland Tel 0800 138 8858)
www.bre.co.uk

Centre for Sustainable Technologies
University of Ulster
Jordanstown
Newtonabbey
N.I. BT37 0QB
Tel. 028 9036 6329

Clean Energy Decision Support Centre
www.retscreen.net
Information, guidance and software downloads for all forms of alternative energy

Energy Saving Trust
21 Dartmouth Street
London SW1H 9BP
Tel 020 7222 0101
www.est.org.uk
List of advice lines for homeowners

Environment Agency
Tel 08708 506 506
www.environment-agency.gov.uk

Green Consumer Guide
www.greenconsumerguide.com
Environmental news

National Energy Foundation
Davy Avenue
Knowlhill
Milton Keynes, MK5 8NG
Tel 01908 665555
www.nef.org.uk

National Renewable Energy Laboratory
www.nrel.gov
Downloads and software for all forms of alternative energy

Recycle Now
www.recyclenow.com
UK based recycling initiative

Renewable Energy UK grant aid
www.clear-skies.org

Thermal Insulation Manufacturers and Suppliers Association (TIMSA)
www.timsa.org.uk

Water Regulations Advisory Scheme
Fern Close
Pen-Y-Fan Industrial Estate
Oakdale
Gwent NP11 3EH
Tel 01495 248454
Email info@wras.co.uk
www.wras.co.uk

Index